Modern Times

Modern France 1870–1976

Barry Williams

Sherborne School for Girls

Longman

LONGMAN GROUP LIMITED

London
*Associated companies, branches and representatives
throughout the world*

First published 1980
ISBN 0 582 22246 X

Set in 10/12pt Baskerville 169
Printed in Hong Kong by Wing Tai Cheung Printing Co. Ltd.

For Pierre and Annick Isidore in Rouen

Acknowledgements

For permission to reproduce photographs we are grateful to the following: Collection Air France, p. 100; Central Press, p. 129; The Condé Nast Publications Ltd, p. 65; E.C.P. Armées, Paris, p. 111; Photo: Equipement, Paris, p. 98 *above* & *below*; French Government Tourist Office, p. 137 (photo: Etienne Revault); Photo Giraudon, p. 44; Illustrated London News Picture Library, p. 6; Keystone, pp. 74, 84, 92, 117, 123, 131; Mansell Collection, pp. 4 *left* & *right*, 17, 26, 46; Musée du Louvre, Paris, p. 34 *above* (photo: Giraudon) and 34 *below* (photo: Lauros-Giraudon); Popperfoto, p. 93; Punch, opposite p. 1, and pp. 28, 49, 56, 136; Musée Rodin, Paris. 'Danaïde' by Rodin in marble, 1885, p. 47. (Photo © Bruno Jarret, Paris); Service Photographique des Archives Nationales, p. 20; Tony Stone Associates Ltd, p. 104; Victoria & Albert Museum, Crown ©, pp. 9, 10, 103 (photo: Cecil Beaton); Collection Viollet, pp. 59, 64 (photo: Boyer Viollet), 70, 72 (photo: Lapi Viollet), 80 (photo: Lapi Viollet), 88 and inset; David & Jill Wright, p. 122

Cover: Novosti Press Agency, Popperfoto, BBC Hulton Picture Library.

Common Ground Filmstrips: *A Portrait of Modern France*
Three filmstrips, in colour, which cover the last 100 years of French history, give a portrait of French society as a whole. Each filmstrip has a set of notes which may be used by the pupils as well as the teacher.
France at the turn of the century; France between the wars; De Gaulle's France

Contents

Part One: New endeavours 1870–1914

1 An End and a Beginning, September 1870   1

2 The Commune   5

3 . . . By One Vote   11

4 L'Affaire Dreyfus   19

5 French Imperialism   29

6 A Portrait of French Society 1871–1914   33

Part Two: France in decline 1914–47

7 'Gentlemen, we shall fight on the Marne'   48

8 Verdun to Versailles   54

9 The 'Twenties   60

10 The 'Thirties: a Dismal Record   67

11 'The Stain of 1940'   77

12 Vichy and the Resistance   84

13 Liberation . . . and 'Collabos' and 'Trafiquants'   90

Part Three: Dynamic revival 1947–76

14 New Confidence and Surging Enterprise 1947–67   97

15 Politicians Argue . . . Meanwhile an Empire Crumbles   107

16 Algeria and the Return of de Gaulle   113

17 Not Everything Prospered   121

18 1968: Crisis Year   128

19 Change and Continuity in the 1970s   134

Index   139

FRANCE, SEPT. 4, 1870.

"AUX ARMES, CITOYENS;
FORMEZ VOS BATAILLONS!"
The "Marseillaise."

Punch cartoon commenting on the news of 4 September: Marianne, symbol of Republican France, urges her followers to arms, recalling the words of the great marching song of the Revolution in the 1790s, the 'Marseillaise'

Part One
New endeavours
1870–1914

1
An End and a Beginning
September 1870

An Empire in Ruins

Early in September 1870 a great battle was fought at Sedan, just inside France's north-eastern frontier. The French suffered the worst defeat in their long history. Emperor Napoleon III and 85,000 men surrendered to the Prusso-German army, and 17,000 Frenchmen died on the field of battle. The French army had been out-numbered, out-generalled and out-manoeuvred. The infantry had fought gallantly and made good use of an efficient new rifle, but their army was badly organised. Troop movements at railway stations were chaotic; stores were rarely where they were wanted; and the French army leaders had issued only maps of Germany to their troops – arrogantly they had never expected to fight the entire war on French soil! With her husband a prisoner and Paris in a state of unrest, the Empress Eugenie fled from the capital disguised as a poor woman on the way to a lunatic asylum. Three days later she was in exile in England. The Second Empire of France was in ruins.

This Franco-Prussian War had been the outcome of a struggle to maintain France's long-held political and military influence on the European continent against the growing power of Germany. In the 1860s one of Germany's thirty-nine separate states, Prussia, led by its minister-president, Otto von Bismarck, began to unite the other states under its leadership. The French Emperor Napoleon III, Eugenie and several of their ministers were determined to make a stand against Germany. Yet on several occasions the Emperor found himself outwitted diplomatically by Bismarck. Finally one French minister said, 'Enough humiliation', and Napoleon, though chronically ill, was persuaded to go to war.

The Birth of the Third French Republic

The news of Sedan reached Paris on 3 September 1870. The next day was beautiful and sunny and people came out onto the streets. An observer, Edmond Goncourt, noted in his diary: 'Crowds moved along the boulevards shouting, "Down with the Empire". There is a wild, tumultuous spectacle of a nation determined to perish or save itself by an enormous effort.' By midday ominous cries of *'Vive la Republique!'* could be heard near the French parliamentary building, the Palais Bourbon. Inside there was confusion. A mob had invaded the debating chamber, where one politician, Jules Favre, called for Napoleon's resignation. Now, with Leon Gambetta, he shouted to the crowd, 'It is not here, but at the Hôtel de Ville that we must proclaim the Republic'. Together they drew off the mob and marched with them eastwards along the banks of the Seine to this famous building, Paris' town hall, where revolutionary governments had been set up in 1789 and 1848. Inside incredible scenes were taking place. Republicans who were more extreme than either Favre or Gambetta had already arrived and were trying to form their own government with the consent of the people. The more moderate new arrivals had to join in a mad scramble for political office. Each leading politician would scribble down lists of a proposed government with his name at the top, then rush to the window and throw them out to the crowds below. According to the cries of *'oui'* or *'non'* a candidate was 'elected'. Favre was frantically trying to keep control for the moderates. He proposed that the new rulers of France should be chosen only from the Paris deputies, and that they should be called the Government of National Defence. The mob approved. At this point Gambetta, with all the dramatic flourish he could muster, stood on a window-sill of the Hôtel de Ville and proclaimed the Third French Republic.

Narrowly, the moderate republicans had kept control. The key posts in the government went to deputies whose political views they knew. Those who would have backed extreme socialist demands for, say, the abolition of property, were kept out. Gambetta persuaded the mobs to accept the tricolour flag of the first great Revolution of 1789-94, not the red flag of the extremists. But one important moderate, Adolphe Thiers, refused office. He said he had no faith in the ideas of this new government, and he was not going to be swayed by the carnival atmosphere that was developing in the warm Parisian sunshine. Within hours the 'men of 4 September', as the government was nicknamed, had to face up to cold realities. The Germans were coming.

Europe Exchanges a Mistress for a Master

After the disaster at Sedan the Prusso-German army expected the French to give in quickly, so they were surprised when Favre declared: 'We shall yield neither an inch of our territory nor a stone of our fortresses.' Gambetta then said it was to be *'guerre à outrance'*, war to the knife.

As the Germans approached, frantic efforts were made to rebuild an army out of what was left of Napoleon III's soldiers by adding a Parisian citizen militia – the National Guard. Normally a small force, this was enlarged to half a million. The soldiers dug earthworks to help the chain of sixteen forts which made a ring of defences for Paris. Food, too, presented difficulties – how long could the city feed a population of two million under siege? The problems facing the new government were enormous, because its members had no practical experience of administration. Most of them had spent a lifetime in opposition to Napoleon III, yet were now catapulted into positions of power, and then only by the consent of the Paris mob. The rest of France had not been consulted. In the event they produced a defence of Paris that won the admiration of the world and even of the German besiegers. For no one thought the siege would last longer than a week, after communications with the rest of France were cut on 23 September. It actually lasted four months, into the depths of one of the worst winters of the century.

Gambetta became a hero of the National Defence when he left Paris in a balloon which floated over the German lines; he then made great efforts to raise a fresh peasant army from rural France. What he could not do was to find efficient officers to lead it. The odds were too great. In January 1871 Paris surrendered – food rationing, smallpox and the German bombardment had eventually made the people of Paris give in. France as a whole was weary of war, and an armistice was arranged until a peace could be negotiated.

Gambetta resigned. Whilst the Germans watched, the French held elections for a new National Assembly: they elected 400 monarchists, compared with only 200 republicans. Everything Gambetta and the moderate republicans had stood for had been rejected, and the provinces of France refused to accept the lead given by their capital city. For one man, Thiers, the elections were a personal triumph. He was the only one amongst the leading politicians who was not directly associated with the disaster at Sedan or with the collapse of the republican effort in Paris. He became the leader of the new government when the National Assembly met at Bordeaux.

Catastrophe at Sedan, surrender of Paris after a long siege – these were bad enough. Yet the French had to put up with two more humiliations. Immediately after the armistice on 18 January 1871 the King of Prussia was proclaimed German Emperor as Kaiser William I, in Louis XIV's great Hall of Mirrors at Versailles. It was a great blow to French pride. A new master, Germany, would henceforth dominate European affairs, having exchanged places with France, once mistress of the continent.

France had to put up with more than this at the signing of the peace treaty in May. Two of her valuable eastern provinces, Alsace and Lorraine, were taken by Germany; a large war indemnity (or compensation) was to be paid by the French; and until it was paid a German army of occupation would remain in the north-east of the country. The loss of Alsace-Lorraine in particular was to embitter Franco-German relations for the next fifty years.

Leon Gambetta, Republican statesman, and hero of the French struggle in the Franco-Prussian War

Adolphe Thiers, eminent statesman of the early years of the Third French republic

2
The Commune

The Guns of Montmartre

Dawn over Paris on Saturday, 18 March 1871 was grey and overcast; there were periods of light, icy rain. The people were disgruntled and edgy, but no one could have forecast that a revolution would begin that day. Events were to be quite spontaneous, some comic, many tragic. On the Butte of Montmartre, the suburb on a steep hill in north-east Paris where it would all begin, the mob violence would be as frightening as it would be unexpected. At the end of the day the Government of France would have given up its right to rule the people of Paris. The seventy-three-day long history of the Paris Commune was about to begin.

The people of Paris had been discontented for a long time. They had many old grievances and suspicions – the slum-dwellers of Belleville and La Villette, just to the east of Montmartre, were bitterly aware of their poverty, and most Parisians had for generations resented any effort by governments to move to the provinces where they felt they would be too much influenced by rural interests. Now the smell of defeat by the Germans was everywhere. Worse still the government decisions from provincial Bordeaux seemed insulting and repressive. First, there was the armistice: 'It is not an armistice, it is a capitulation', warned the extreme republican newspaper *Rappel*, 'Paris is trembling with anger.' Its acceptance by the French Assembly at Bordeaux ('an assembly of country-bumpkins', one Parisian called it), and the humiliating peace terms which followed, heaped injury upon injury. Secondly, the Germans had been allowed to make a triumphal march through Paris: 'What shame, what dishonour these royalists have brought upon our country', a republican wrote. Thirdly, in the Assembly of 768 deputies, over 400 were monarchists, and when they moved from Bordeaux to Versailles with its royalist-Bourbon associations, republicans in Paris were alarmed. They regarded the republican form of government as having been settled on that hectic September day five months before. Finally the government now insisted that all commercial bills should be paid immediately – shopkeepers' debts had of course been impossible to settle during the long winter siege, but to expect such prompt payment seemed insensitive.

Two more actions by the government showed its incompetence. The National Guards, Paris' own citizen militia, had their pay stopped immediately the armistice was confirmed in February. Then, in March, the government decided that the army should take back over 400 cannons, which the Guards had removed from the big artillery parks around Paris to prevent them being seized by the Germans as war booty – 171 of them had been hauled up to the 'safe' area of the Butte of Montmartre. In the eyes of Adolphe Thiers, who had come to Paris to see this was done, both acts were practical. The country could not afford to pay local soldiers who were not needed.

So, through the cold, misty rain at three am on the 18 March, two generals led several thousand soldiers of the French regular army up to Montmartre. Apart from a few sentries who were easily overpowered, the people of Montmartre were fast asleep. Within an hour the government troops had the guns under their control.

However, the troops soon realised that someone had bungled. Horses were needed to haul the artillery away – but no one had thought to bring any. Whilst they were sent for, the soldiers sat and waited. Montmartre slowly came to life. Women came out and began to argue with the soldiers: where did they think they were taking the guns – to

The guns which defended Paris against the Germans being dragged to safety on the heights of Montmartre

Berlin? Bread and wine were offered to the cold and hungry troöps, who now no longer saw any point in Thiers' operation. Gradually as the day wore on thousands of women and National Guards moved into Montmartre. Georges Clemenceau, future premier of France, now the young mayor of the district, wrote later, 'The mob was in the grip of some kind of frenzy. All were shrieking like wild beasts.' The two generals were seized and killed by the mob in the afternoon. There was going to be no quiet, orderly removal of the guns now. Elsewhere in Paris the loyalty of the National Guards was fast evaporating: of the 400,000 Guardsmen only about 6,000, mainly respectable *bourgeoisie*, could be counted on to support the Government. At three pm Thiers and the few of his ministers who were in Paris at the time decided to leave. Some made hasty exits for Versailles in coaches driven at full gallop; the regular soldiers had to march out, while amazed Parisians jeered at them. For the moment the city was left to the revolutionaries.

The Commune's Personalities and Policies

The Hôtel de Ville immediately became the centre of heated debates. Who should now rule Paris? What form of government should be set up? The outward form was soon settled. Elections were arranged for a new town council of ninety members, and at the end of March the members were wildly cheered by Parisians at the official opening ceremony. 'In the name of the people, the Commune is proclaimed', was shouted over the roar of the crowd, 'Vive la Commune'. But the rejoicing concealed widely different hopes for the future. Some groups, especially the *petit bourgeoisie* of small shopkeepers, looked forward to moderate reforms now that at last there was a real commune for Paris. Despite Thiers' fears, there was nothing basically revolutionary about a commune: it simply meant independence for a town, whereby its people could make their own laws and administer their own taxes – independent, said one member, of that 'pack of peasants in the Assembly who normally control France'. But only a quarter of the council could be called moderates.

Other groups, however, did see in the Commune a chance to introduce revolutionary ideas. The Blanquists were socialists who hated any control from a central government, and particularly wanted to get rid of the Roman Catholic Church and the army. Their leader was Auguste Blanqui, nicknamed the 'Spider of Revolution'; he had spent twenty-eight of his sixty-six years of life in various prisons. The Jacobins, led by another old, ill and tragic figure, Delescluze, were passionate admirers of the great days of the Jacobin dictatorship under Robespierre in 1794.

These groups were not organised parties, and there were many capable individuals claiming attention at the Commune meetings. One of the most colourful members was Louise Michel, who became a familiar figure, wearing a huge red belt and carrying a fixed-bayoneted rifle, stalking through Paris demanding money for ambulances and medical supplies.

These men and women now settled down to 'govern' Paris. They made no immediate effort to approach Thiers at Versailles, but few of their actions were at all revolutionary. They did not seize the Bank of France, for instance; in fact, a methodical and honest book-keeper named Jourde ran the Commune's finances, and he negotiated a loan for the Commune from the Bank! Practical reforms were popular like the abolition of night-work in bakeries and of fines in workshops, and the limiting of Commune members' salaries to that of an average workman.

But the Commune was mainly concerned with the problems of food and defence. It was most unlikely that Thiers would accept the Commune's 'declaration of independence' permanently. Within weeks Paris was to be faced with a second siege – this time by Frenchmen. The Commune hoped to defeat Thiers' troops by using a massive force of Parisian conscripts. The reality proved disastrous, however, for there was no proper planning of a campaign, and communications and medical services – despite Louise Michel – were in a desperate muddle.

La Semaine Sanglante, 21–28 May 1871

The Commune did have some weeks of peace. If anything government at Versailles was in a worse muddle than the Commune at the Hôtel de Ville. The French Assembly, one observer remarked, was 'fiddling while Paris burned'. To be fair to Thiers he needed time to regroup and discipline his forces. He kept up a steady bombardment of parts of Paris, reducing a western suburb, Neuilly, almost to rubble. The real onslaught came on 21 May. Delescluze called the Commune troops to the barricades, proclaiming: 'The hour of revolutionary warfare has struck'. But there was no coherent defence of the city. As the Versailles troops poured in through the gates of Paris, Parisians retreated hastily, each person determined to defend his own street.

A week of terrible bloodshed – *la semaine sanglante* – followed. The real horrors of civil war were revealed. Both sides took hostages and shot them, including the Archbishop of Paris; some of Paris' finest buildings (the Tuileries, the Palais de Justice, the Hôtel de Ville) were demolished. For a week the Commune fought against enormous odds, but in the end Paris was subjugated. The repression that followed was ruthless. A newspaper recorded, 'One could see on the Seine a long streak of blood flowing with the current.' Several French historians today agree that between 20,000 and 25,000 died. It was a staggering total. No single battle of the Prussian War had cost so many lives.

Karl Marx and Myths of the Commune

Powerful myths about the Commune were created in 1871 that historians have since disproved or declared exaggerated. One of them, that the Communards behaved like savages, led newspapers to demand that they be slaughtered to a man. The harsh measures that the government took against the Communards caused a rift between the *bourgeoisie* and the workers which slowed down the reform of the

Supporters of the Commune were regarded as traitors. This painting shows Communards suffering speedy execution

The Hôtel de Ville, where the Republic had been proclaimed in 1870, now in ruins after being gutted by fire in the Commune fighting

workers' conditions for decades. They also made the people of Paris and the people in the rural areas of France very suspicious of each other, and some say that this suspicion still exists today. A few days after the Commune was crushed, Karl Marx, author of the 1848 'Communist Manifesto' and already a well-known revolutionary, wrote a book about the Commune called 'The Civil War in France' which many people read. Today French people still argue about the Commune and take sides, but they remember what Marx said about the Commune rather than what it actually was. He wrote that the Commune was 'essentially a working-class government', and that the seventy-three-day episode was a 'glorious forerunner of a new society'. He was quite wrong. Only twenty-five members of the Commune were manual workers; the others were bourgeois doctors, teachers, lawyers and journalists. Nor was the Commune a socialist government: many of its members were inspired more by memories of the 1789 Revolution than by any vision of a socialist future! And it is worth noting that a member of the Commune was called a 'communard' not a 'communist'.

Yet myths often have considerable power to influence men's minds. Inside France, Thiers' equation that 'the Commune = Socialism' poisoned relations between the well-to-do and the poorer workers for more than a generation. Much later, in 1964, the continuing power of the myth was shown when Soviet astronauts took three souvenirs into space: two pictures of Marx and Lenin, and a ribbon from a Communard flag.

3
. . . By One Vote

'Three men can't sit on it'

The Republic, so dramatically proclaimed by the 'men of 4 September' in 1870, had no legal backing. The Bordeaux National Assembly was elected in 1871 only to make peace with Germany and then to settle the future form of France's government, so it clearly had a limited life; and Thiers' leadership of the government was recognised by all as equally temporary. So, was there any way this republican constitution could be made permanent? It seemed unlikely: the Assembly had its majority of monarchists; Thiers was known as a moderate constitutional royalist; and the republicans, who regularly argued bitterly with each other across the debating floor of the Assembly, had small chance of getting their policies accepted. People now regarded Gambetta, hero of the winter of 1870, as being too revolutionary – a 'disturber of the peace who ought to be locked up', wrote one newspaper.

Yet those who wished to see an end to the Republic could not agree amongst themselves.[1] A few imperialists still hoped for the return of another Bonaparte. Two branches of the old royal house of France attracted much loyalty. Henri, Comte de Chambord, of the Bourbon line, had the great seventeenth-century names of Henri IV and Louis XIV behind him, and was already being referred to as Henri V by his supporters. The Comte de Paris of the Orléanist line had had his ancestor Louis Philippe more recently on the throne. Thiers put the problem bluntly to the Assembly in 1873: 'There is only one throne; three men can't sit on it'.

The problem on paper was easily solved. Chambord was fifty-six and childless; Orléans was thirty-five with a growing family – so Chambord should immediately become king with the Comte de Paris as his heir. But Henri, Comte de Chambord was stubborn. He insisted on having the white flag of the old Bourbon kings, instead of the tricolour flag of the Revolution of 1789. The red, white and blue tricolour had stood for the end of privilege and for the principles of *Liberté, egalité et fraternité;* people felt that if Chambord rejected the flag, he might also go back on

[1]See the guide on page 14

these principles. One of his official statements gave little hope of compromise: 'I do not wish to become King of the Revolution.'

Thiers, who had rendered great service to France by organising massive loans to pay off the German indemnity, came to believe that the republican form of government should be retained. He reluctantly admitted, 'It divides us least.' But the monarchists in the Assembly seemed content to play a waiting game. Thiers, no longer their champion, was dismissed and Marshal MacMahon became President of the Republic. Though a staunch royalist, he was little else: easily bored by politics, he was thought to be rather stupid. (A newspaper was prosecuted for publishing a cartoon of MacMahon seated on a horse, with the caption, 'The Horse looks intelligent'!) However, others besides Thiers began to tire of the arguments and uncertainty. 1875 proved a crucial year.

For: 353   Against: 352

January 1875 began with yet more political manoeuvrings in the National Assembly. Early on, one of a series of votes on a possible constitution used the word 'republic' in it, and it was easily defeated. But there were no organised parties in the Assembly and in the shifting sands of political opinion the Orléanists, suddenly worried that the Bonapartists were gaining ground, sided temporarily with the republicans. On 30 January a vote was taken on a motion called the Wallon Amendment, which included the sentence: 'The President of the Republic is elected . . . for seven years'.. It was carried by 353 to 352. The republicans were jubilant. The monarchists, preoccupied with the Bonapartists, failed to realise that they had not voted for a temporary, seven-year president, but for a permanent office to be filled every seven years. The republican form of government had at last been legally accepted. A royalist later lamented at 'such a burlesque ending' to a serious problem. Others insisted they had not properly understood what they were voting for, and it couldn't last long anyway. Yet the Republic was to last until 1940.

It was a remarkable event: the Third French Republic was thus legally founded by a monarchist assembly, with a royalist President and royalist ministers in office, on the motion of Wallon, a Catholic lawyer who insisted later he had not been asking for a permanent republic; the motion was passed by the narrowest of majorities, one – and one deputy who was against the Amendment arrived minutes too late to vote!

Seize Mai 1877

In the 1876 elections the country showed its approval of the Republic. The monarchists lost badly, republicans ending up with a 2:1 advantage. An awkward political situation had arisen. France now had a very conservative, royalist president (MacMahon), but a republican assembly intent on reform. The constitutional laws under which the Republic was governed had intended making the president a strong figure: he was elected for seven years, and he could choose his own cabinet. Yet he was expected to have the 'confidence' of the majority of the Chamber of Deputies. President MacMahon started a major political row when, on 16 May 1877, he forced the chief minister to resign and then dissolved the Assembly after only one year. Huge efforts were made by the monarchists in the elections which followed to ensure that another republican assembly was not returned. Tours and speeches were made all over France; the local gentry, town officials and the Catholic Church supported MacMahon; republican newspapers and even café meeting-places were closed down, but to no avail. The election following the crisis of *seize mai* returned nearly as many republicans as before. MacMahon soon resigned. He had lost the struggle to ensure the President held firm control over the affairs of the nation.

A significant change had taken place. Socially, huge numbers of traditionally conservative voters throughout rural France had refused to be dictated to by the well-to-do landowners and priests. Politically, power passed from the President and his ministers to the Chamber of Deputies. The latter was an ominous development. As there were no organised and disciplined political parties, and as elections did not have to follow the fall of a government, governments became weak coalitions which were easily defeated in the Assembly, often on minor issues. Prime ministers were mainly colourless figures, and only rarely over the next forty years were strong politicians like Gambetta, Jules Ferry and Georges Clemenceau in top office – Clemenceau, in fact, became well known as 'the overthrower of cabinets'. Perhaps the real weakness of French political life can be shown by adding up the number of cabinet governments: between 1870 and 1940 there were 108, an average length of eight months per ministry (in Britain between 1801 and 1937, i.e. twice the time, there were only forty-four, with an average length of three years).

Politics in France: a brief, simplified guide to help the reader

Pre–1870: Three political traditions

1 Royalist

From early medieval times until the French Revolution of 1789–94 France had a monarchy and only the king had the power to make decisions. The monarchy was restored in 1814 (the Bourbon and later Orleanist Houses) and remained in power until 1848.

2 Republican

During the First Republic, 1792–1804, and the Second Republic, 1848–52, power was transferred from the monarchy to a parliament of elected representatives. This type of government was often referred to as 'Sovereignty of the People'.

3 Imperial or Bonapartist

Under Napoleon I (1804–14/15) and Napoleon III (1852–70) France was ruled by the House of Bonaparte, which based its authority on great personal and military prestige.

1870 to the present day: Institutions and Positions of Power

Executive: the government of the President, his Prime Minister and Cabinet of Ministers, who decide on a policy and, if it is approved by the legislature, see that it is carried out. Sometimes advised by a Council of State.

Legislature: the elected representives of the people in a parliament of two houses: the Senate and the National Assembly (sometimes called the Chamber of Deputies).

President: works from his official residence in the Elysée Palace in Paris. He appoints the prime minister with the approval of the National Assembly. He can dissolve a particular National Assembly and call new elections after consultation with his prime minister and leading Senate members, but he rarely uses this power. Presidential elections are usually held every 7 years.

	Third Republic		Vichy Regime		Provision
1870	←————————→	1940	←————————→	1944	←———

National Assembly: 465 Deputies (plus some from French territories overseas) elected by a system of proportional representation. Over 75 % of the electorate vote regularly, elections always taking place on Sunday, normally every 5 years. The Assembly meets in Palais Bourbon in Paris, in a room with semi-cirular tiers of seats facing a rostrum from which all speeches are made.

The Third, Fourth and Fifth Republics differ in the amount of power exercised by each of these institutions.

From 1877 real power in the Third Republic and Fourth Republic was in the hands of the National Assembly, and the President and Cabinet of Ministers were rather like figureheads.

Since 1958 real power in the Fifth Republic has been in the hands of the President, who exercises decisive and active leadership, while the power of the National Assembly has been reduced.

Some important points to remember (particularly where they contrast with British practice)

French politics is very much a matter of personalities – elections, policies and party discipline are far less important than they are in Britain.

There are many parties and loose political groupings; every government is therefore a coalition which tends to be less stable than a one-party government.

A serious defeat of a government means that a new prime minister must form a new government; but a new election need not take place and often there is little real change in policy.

For local government France has 90 (93 since 1965) departments (similar to counties in England) each administered by an elected council working with a prefect, a permanent official chosen by the central government in Paris. He has real power in education, tax collection and social welfare. The smallest local government council is the commune, which has a mayor who works closely with the prefect. France has 34,000 communes.

Govt.	Fourth Republic	Fifth Republic
➝1946 ⟵	⟵———————————➝1958 ⟵	———————————➝

Consolidation

The republicans decided that, to maintain their new-found support, they would have to keep their policies fairly moderate. As Gambetta remarked, 'the Republic has planted her feet in the peasants' *sabots* [clogs] and she will not cast them off.' He meant that it became a conservative republic, introducing its policies very slowly.

Some policies were symbolic and showed the nostalgia for 1789. For instance, the government declared that *La Marseillaise*, that stirring marching-song of the Great Revolution, should become the French national anthem and that the date the Bastille was stormed, 14 July, should be a national holiday. Gambetta, on humanitarian grounds as well as to silence noisy socialist complaints, persuaded the Assembly to allow exiled Communards to return to France. They arrived in 1879–80 having suffered rough treatment in French colonial prisons, many sick, all in rags.

The government put through reforms which gave important liberties and opportunities to the masses of French people. It granted freedom of the press in 1881, established the right to set up trade unions three years later, and introduced a law permitting divorce. It made education in state-supported primary schools free and later compulsory. But an important freedom, the right of people to assemble in public without government control, did not come until 1907. The Assembly discussed social welfare programmes but made very little headway because of the cost.

The prime minister, Jules Ferry, made the republican control of the Assembly and central government doubly sure by ending the centuries-old domination of provincial government by the landowning aristocracy. From 1884 mayors had to be freely elected by the local councils. The mayor had the real power in French villages: his duty was to carry out state laws and his influence was very great. The local constable, tax collector, innkeeper, schoolmaster and even tobacconist, for example, depended on him for their positions and licences. Together the mayors formed a powerful group at election time, and now the politicians of the Third Republic were able to keep this group on their side.

Despite all these efforts to get more support, many of the Republic's political leaders lived in fear of the old forces in French society. These anti-republicans could still be found in important positions as judges, as officials of the administration, in the Roman Catholic Church and particularly in the senior ranks of the army. It had happened before: the first great Napoleon Bonaparte had seized power through the army from the First French Republic and Directory in the late 1790s. Many wondered whether a general-on-horseback could return to challenge the Third Republic.

Boulanger

In January 1886 General Georges Boulanger, thought to be one of the few liberals in the army, was appointed Minister of War in the French government. The army, with new ideas for conscription instead of relying purely on a professional body of men, needed overhauling, and Boulanger set about his task energetically and with success. Quickly people began to hear about this man with a flair for publicity. By 14 July he was the darling of the Parisian crowds, when, mounted on a huge black horse, he led a dazzling military parade at Longchamps in

General Boulanger

western Paris. Within twelve months he was calling the French Assembly inefficient, and demanding a more powerful presidency. Boulanger was dismissed from office, but relying on his popularity and on some convenient revelations of government corruption, he put himself up as a candidate in a series of by-elections. In January 1889 he stood in a Paris election and gained an overwhelming victory – crowds there appealed to Boulanger to march to the President's palace and seize power.

But Boulanger ignored cries by the Paris mob of 'á l'Elysée'. There seems little doubt that on that one evening he could have become master of Paris, and was urged to act by his friends. But he drew back at the last minute. When he learned he might be charged with conspiracy to overthrow the Government, he fled to Belgium, and later committed suicide beside the grave of his mistress.

Though the episode ended in farce it had been a dangerous moment for the republicans – not only had all the old conservative-monarchists supported Boulanger, but so had the fickle Parisian masses. The anti-republicans were to use the power of the newspapers to whip up mass feelings to produce many more scandals and crises which threatened the stability of the Republic. No sooner had the Boulanger episode died down, than a fresh problem appeared. Ferdinand de Lesseps, who had successfully planned the Suez Canal, tried to repeat his triumph with a Panama Canal. But millions of francs of investors' money was lost in a vain effort to cut through the hills and mosquito-ridden swamps of central America. De Lesseps' company went bankrupt, and investigations revealed that huge bribes had been paid to leading government figures to support the project. This scandal was followed in the 1890s by the most bizarre episode in modern French history. This time the enemies of the Republic seized upon the astonishing affair of Captain Alfred Dreyfus.

4
L'Affaire Dreyfus

The Dreyfus affair was so dramatic that it seemed like a five-act tragedy, with all the tensions, suspicions, bitterness and clashes of powerful personalities that one associates with theatrical drama. Its 'cast' was huge; the leading 'actors' were:

CAPTAIN ALFRED DREYFUS – born in 1859 in Alsace, a Jewish artillery officer, temporarily attached to French Army Intelligence

MATHIEU DREYFUS – Alfred's brother

MAITRE EDGAR DEMANGE – Dreyfus' lawyer at the 1894 and 1899 trials

LIEUTENANT-COLONEL GEORGES PICQUART – Head of French Intelligence in 1896

GEORGES CLEMENCEAU – outspoken editor of *L'Aurore* newspaper, and future premier of France

EMILE ZOLA – author with a reputation in France similar to Dickens or Shaw in Britain

MAJOR HUBERT HENRY – member of the Intelligence Service section in the French War Office

GENERAL AUGUSTE MERCIER – Minister of War at the time of the 1894 trial

GENERAL GODEFROY CAVAIGNAC – Minister of War at the time of the 1899 trial

EDOUARD DRUMONT – editor of *La Libre Parole* newspaper

JEAN DUBOIS – clerk in the map office of the French War Ministry in 1894

MAJOR (LATER COLONEL) FERDINAND ESTERHAZY – an infantry regimental commander in the French army

COLONEL MAX VON SCHWARTZKOPPEN – chief military attaché at the German Embassy in Paris

COLONEL PANIZZARDI – chief military attaché at the Italian Embassy in Paris.

ACT ONE: In Which the Central Document of L'Affaire is Revealed and Alfred Dreyfus is Court-Martialled

Late in September 1894 Major Henry, who worked in counter-espionage at the French Army Intelligence Service in the rue St Dominique in Paris, brought to the notice of his superior officers a *bordereau*. This was a form listing the documents in a file, and in this case was handwritten with some personal comments; it had been torn across. Henry said he had received it from an informer working in the German Embassy in Paris who had found the *bordereau* in the waste-paper basket of Colonel Schwartzkoppen. The listed information suggested that someone in the French army had passed on a file of military secrets to the Germans. Among the interesting words on the *bordereau* were:

'I am sending you some information,
1 A note on the 120 . . . [a new French field-gun]
3 The note on a modification in artillery formations . . .
5 The Firing Manual of Field Artillery . . .
I am just off on manoeuvres.'

The *bordereau* was shown to the Minister of War, General Mercier, who was naturally alarmed that a spy should have access to secret and vital matters. A handwriting investigation followed. Only a limited number of officers could have had access to such information, each section of which could be found in four quite different parts of the War Ministry; thus it was probably an officer on a training course who had spent a few months in each of the four parts. Suspicion fell on a Captain Dreyfus because the 't' and 'i' in the word *'artillerie'* looked similar to his handwriting. Two experts disagreed on the handwriting judgement, but Mercier had already decided to arrest Dreyfus. Early on Monday 15 October he was taken into custody, whilst his trial was prepared. Dreyfus, firmly denying any treachery, found himself with few supporters. He was a cold, rather aloof man, born in Alsace (under German rule since 1871), and the son of a rich Jewish textile

The bordereau, the document which started it all in September 1894

manufacturer. His personality and his Jewish-Alsatian background made him unpopular and an easy target for suspicions. In the five weeks before the trial two important developments occurred. First, a dossier was prepared on Dreyfus which contained the *bordereau* and many other scraps of information that had been found in French Intelligence files. One of these scraps was part of a letter from Schwartzkoppen to Panizzardi in the Italian Embassy: it said, 'Enclosed are twelve maps of Nice that scoundrel D. left with me for you.' Secondly, the press found out and began a sensational campaign against Dreyfus. Major Henry sent some information to Edouard Drumont, the editor of an extremely anti-Jewish newspaper, *La Libre Parole*. The paper stated publicly, 'The miserable, shameful officer who has sold the secrets is Captain Dreyfus. There is absolute proof that he has sold our secrets to Germany.' General Mercier too was so convinced of Dreyfus' guilt that he declared to an important French daily newspaper, *Le Figaro*, 'that for more than three years Dreyfus was in contact with a foreign power'. The campaign against Dreyfus was now taken up by a Catholic newspaper *La Croix*: 'Dreyfus is an agent of international Jewry which has decided to ruin the French people.' Public interest intensified. One newspaper said Dreyfus was a gambler, another that he had a mistress in Nice who was an Italian spy. Money and love were motives that people would easily understand.

When Dreyfus appeared at his court-martial, he was virtually a condemned man. The trial itself was quite sensational. Major Henry, in giving evidence, dramatically pointed to Dreyfus and shouted, 'The traitor, there he is.' Then the dossier on Dreyfus was secretly passed to the judge; the defence lawyer, Maître Demange, was not allowed to see it. In such conditions the verdict was obvious: guilty. He was sentenced to life imprisonment on the dreaded Devil's Island, off the South American coast. Before being sent there, there was a public military ceremony in which his officer decorations and sword were torn off and broken. Whilst Dreyfus cried, 'I am innocent; vive la France', the watching crowd shouted back, 'Death to the Jew!'

For the army *L'affaire Dreyfus* was finished.

ACT TWO: In Which Doubts are Raised, a New Document is Found and . . . Enter Major Esterhazy, a Possible Villain

Demange refused to accept the verdict. He protested at the secret dossier and its use at the trial, but the army pleaded the need for military security. Dreyfus' brother, Mathieu, denounced the press campaign. He was told by Demange, 'If Captain Dreyfus was not Jewish he would not be in prison.' More serious, however, were questions which arose about the whole judicial process. Assumptions had been made about the *bordereau*. Would Schwartzkoppen have been so careless as to throw it away into a wastepaper basket? Was Dreyfus the only man to have access to the information in the secret dossier? (A clerk in the War Ministry map office, Jean Dubois, would know about the Nice fortifications, but this was not thought important because of his junior rank.) Again, the *bordereau* was only a list; if the file's contents were only outline descriptions, then perhaps others could have known. But the more Mathieu Dreyfus tried to investigate, the more alarm he created: army officers regarded him as a rich, but dangerous, Jew.

There the matter might have rested, had not a new figure, Colonel Picquart, become head of the French Intelligence Service. He was not particularly interested in Dreyfus and was known to dislike Jews, but in the spring of 1896 another document was brought to him from the Schwartzkoppen waste-paper basket. This was an undelivered *petit-bleu*, a kind of letter-telegram. Part of it said: 'To Major Count Esterhazy – I await a more detailed explanation than you gave me the other day on the matter in question . . .' Curious thoughts occurred to Picquart. Why had Schwarzkoppen not sent the *petit-bleu?* Surely he would not have carelessly thrown away yet another 'spy' document. Anyway, it was only a suspicious note, not proof of anything. The results of Picquart's discreet enquiries into Major Esterhazy were odder still. He was commander of a French army regiment at Rouen; his handwriting seemed very like that of the *bordereau;* he was a gambler, and was known to spend lavishly on several lady-friends; he had once served in French Intelligence, and one of his personal friends was Major Henry.

These enquiries took a long time, and Picquart made himself very unpopular with his fellow-officers. A general told him bluntly, 'The Dreyfus case is closed.' A critical point came in November 1896: Henry 'found' a letter which seemed to make nonsense of all Picquart's suspicions. It was a note from Panizzardi to Schwarzkoppen urging that 'no one must ever know what happened', and in it Dreyfus's name was spelt out in full. To the army officers the conclusion was obvious: Dreyfus was certainly guilty, and the Esterhazy information was only coincidence. It was Picquart now whose investigations alarmed his senior officers – he was quickly posted to Tunisia.

Picquart was not to be silenced so easily, however. He revealed some of his suspicions to a few members of the French National Assembly. Press interest, too, had revived. Various army secrets had been leaked, including a photograph of the *bordereau*. For Mathieu Dreyfus and Demange, Picquart's discovery of the *petit-bleu* was exactly what they had been waiting for. Late in 1897 Mathieu publicly denounced Esterhazy as a traitor.

Events moved swiftly but disastrously for Dreyfus' supporters. Esterhazy vigorously denied such allegations; he demanded his own trial in order to clear his name, and this was granted. On 11 January 1898, after army evidence stating that Esterhazy could not possibly have known the details in the *bordereau* file, the judges took only three minutes to acquit him. The *petit-bleu* was ignored. The next day Picquart, having been brought back from Tunisia, was arrested and later dismissed from the army in disgrace. For those convinced of Dreyfus' original guilt, Act Two was brought to a triumphal close.

Their expectation that *L'Affaire* was now indeed over was short-lived. It was about to become a national issue, dividing even families.

ACT THREE: 'J'Accuse' – in Which the Intervention of a Famous Novelist Turns a Private Tragedy into a Sensational National Controversy

On 13 January 1898, a mere forty-eight hours after Esterhazy's acquittal, the newspaper *L'Aurore* published a letter which Emile Zola had just written to the President of the French Republic. Zola was a famous novelist with a world-wide reputation. The letter, boldly headed, 'I Accuse', was a violent and scathing attack on the army. Generals like Mercier were named, and accused first of deliberately framing Dreyfus, and then of ordering the acquittal of Esterhazy.

L'Aurore was the radical newspaper of Georges Clemenceau, who had been Mayor of Montmartre in the Commune days. He had printed Zola's letter because he felt the Republic was in danger. Behind the army, Zola argued, stood all the enemies of the Republic: the privileged classes, royalists, the power of the Catholic Church – all of them infected by horrible anti-semitism (that attitude of mind which hates all Jews). It was a vicious attack on the aristocracy of France. Such accusations could not be ignored. Zola even demanded that he be tried in court so that he could justify them. Early in February thousands crowded in icy weather around the court-house, where Zola's tumultuous trial was to last two weeks.

Everyone's attention was focused on the trial. What before had merely been a spy affair, conducted mostly behind a military wall of silence, with the newspapers only guessing from scraps of information, now became a national issue. Amidst mounting tension, in which Zola's lawyers tried to re-open the whole Dreyfus question, one exasperated general said openly that a crucial document (Henry's Panizzardi letter of November 1896) proved Dreyfus' guilt. Another put the whole reputation of the army at stake:

'You, gentlemen of the jury, are the nation. If the nation has no confidence in the leaders of the Army, in those responsible for national defence, then the leaders are ready to give up their heavy duty.'

It seemed that the 'nation' had to choose between Dreyfus and the army. 'J'Accuse', a contemporary said, 'was decisive. It compelled everyone to take sides in the struggle.'

On the one side stood the Anti-Dreyfusards, as they were called. The army officers saw their honour and prestige at stake. Since the defeat of 1871 they had been very sensitive to 'spy-mania'. Foreign agents, Jews and unscrupulous republican politicians had to be carefully watched, for they were the 'enemy within' who might undermine French national security. With the army was the Catholic Church – anti-semitic and suspicious of the Third Republic and its political ideas. Many priests came from a peasant background, and in many village communities Jews were the outsiders, to be laughed at, despised or hated. Royalists too supported the army, with a pretender to the throne of France ready to step in if the Republic should fall.

On the other side, the Dreyfusards were fighting a difficult battle. They took their stand on the traditions of the 1789 Revolution, the ideals of justice and individual rights. Zola had concluded his letter with a clarion call, 'Truth is on the march and nothing will stop it.' Both the army and the Catholic Church seemed to be claiming so much power that republican politicians saw them as a threat to the very existence of the government.

When Zola was found guilty and sentenced to one year's imprisonment it was evident that the Dreyfusards were losing the struggle. All this time, of course, Alfred Dreyfus remained in prison, ignorant of what had been going on; in the melée of the events leading up to Zola's trial, the guilt or innocence of the central character in the affair seemed to have been forgotten.

ACT FOUR: In Which a Forgery is Revealed . . . to be Followed by a Suicide, and a Hurried Departure

The army officers had won. But they were over-confident. Mercier retired, and a new War Minister, General Cavaignac, determined to end the Dreyfus agitation once and for all. Convinced of Dreyfus' guilt, he decided to prove it in a speech in July 1898 to the French Assembly by producing some of the key documents. His outstanding proof was the letter of November 1896. For the first time Panizzardi's letter to Schwartzkoppen, naming Dreyfus, was read out aloud in full and later printed in the newspapers. Colonel Picquart, who had suffered so much in his support of justice, returned to the attack: he told the press that the letter 'had the appearance of a forgery'. Cavaignac asked for a special check to be made, and one of his officers made a dramatic discovery late at night on 13 August 1898. The strong light of his reading lamp revealed the centre part of Panizzardi's letter – the segment containing Dreyfus' name – to be a forgery. Events once more moved swiftly. Colonel Henry, who had brought the document to light, was questioned; caught in a trap, he confessed. He was arrested, but slit his own throat whilst awaiting trial. Meanwhile, Major Esterhazy fled via Belgium to London. Cavaignac resigned. The whole basis of the anti-Dreyfusard case was collapsing.

ACT FIVE: In Which Captain Alfred Dreyfus is Re-tried – Twice

There was mounting pressure for the complete re-examination of the Dreyfus trial and its evidence. The *bordereau* was once more inspected and the possibility that Esterhazy had written it accepted. The government agreed to the re-trial of Dreyfus. He was brought back from Devil's Island in 1899. Over four years of solitary confinement had taken a heavy toll. He was ill, and found difficulty in talking. He knew little of the developments since 1895. A fresh trial was prepared at Rennes in Brittany – well away from the emotional atmosphere of Paris.

The Dreyfusards were confident of success, but the affair still had some dramatic twists. Dreyfus entered the court-room on 7 August 1899, 'an old, old man of 39', an observer noted. The same evidence as in 1895 was again presented and repeated as if time had somehow given it an extra truth. His lawyer, Maître Demange, again found himself up against information only at the disposal of the army. Once more, 'proof', one way or the other, got lost. Appeals to commonsense by the defence were met by army officers piling one piece of circumstantial evidence on another. A remark, for instance, by Dreyfus, that he was 'known to some Germans' was taken as added proof of guilt. For the army, treason and national security were the great issues: suspicion was enough. The verdict of the judges, by five to two, was again guilty, but this time with special circumstances. Dreyfus' life imprisonment was reduced to ten years.

The leading members of the government of the Third Republic were by now convinced that justice was not being done. With the royalist-catholic backing the army was getting, they felt they had to act. The

Caption Alfred Dreyfus: an artist's impression at the Rennes trial of 1899

President offered a pardon. It was not proof of innocence, but Dreyfus, in bad health, accepted it, and quietly slipped away into the country to live with his sister.

It was an anti-climax. The public soon became bored; newspapers had other interesting things to consider. But *l'Affaire* would haunt the political life of France for many years: it was a symptom of the ease with which rivalries in French society could be exploited.

At the personal level, Dreyfus' friends continued to work to prove his innocence, on the grounds that previous courts had been misled by false evidence. It was a long, slow process. Finally in 1906 an Appeal Court set up by the government examined all the evidence. For the first time some revealing new testimony was given: four artillery officers, who had never been consulted, declared that the *bordereau* could not have been written by an artillery officer – it was too vague; and more importantly the outline information on the 120 mm gun had been available at a special army meeting in 1894, which Dreyfus had not attended, but Esterhazy had. Alfred Dreyfus was at last proved innocent. In an emotional scene for all Dreyfusards, he was re-instated in the army and awarded the Legion of Honour.

Postscript: Who Then was Guilty?

Dreyfus served his country well in the First World War, and died quietly in retirement in 1935. Picquart became a general, but died in 1914. Zola had died in 1902. Of the other key figures, Mercier died in 1921 believing to the end he said that Dreyfus was guilty. Esterhazy remained in exile in London under another name until his death in 1923.

Then in 1931 the private papers of Max von Schwartzkoppen, who had died in 1917, were published. They revealed that Esterhazy was indeed the key spy and author of the *bordereau*. The *petit-bleu* had been written by Schwartzkoppen, and he had been very careless in throwing away such documents. The 'D' of the Italian letter was not Dreyfus, but Dubois, the man originally considered but thought to be too minor. Yet *L'Affaire* still has its mysteries. A legend has grown up of a third man, a mysterious 'Monsieur X', who was the real organiser behind Esterhazy. For instance, it has been suggested that Esterhazy was a double agent in General Mercier's employ who sold worthless information to the Germans; for the Germans to remain hoodwinked Dreyfus had to suffer. It seems unlikely that the entire truth will ever be known.

MARCHEZ! MARCHAND!

GENERAL JOHN BULL (*to* MAJOR MARCHAND). "COME, PROFESSOR, YOU'VE HAD A NICE LITTLE
SCIENTIFIC TRIP! I'VE SMASHED THE DERVISHES—LUCKILY FOR *YOU*—AND NOW I RECOMMEND
YOU TO PACK UP YOUR FLAGS, AND GO HOME!!!"

*British patriotism and arrogance in 1898. Marchand at Fashoda in the Sudan is politely but
firmly told to get out*

5
French Imperialism

The Conquest of an Empire

The old French Empire, with its interests in Canada, India and the West Indies, was lost in the long struggle with Great Britain in the eighteenth century. Only scattered fragments, mainly decaying trading posts, remained by 1830. Then, in that year, a small settlement was established in Algeria, and later some new trading posts were added in West Africa and in south-east Asia. This was the base on which Frenchmen created one of the greatest colonial empires in the world between 1880 and 1914.

The story of its creation is simply told. In Algeria Frenchmen sought possession of what was said to be one of the great fertile areas in the world. But it took twenty years of warfare with a variety of native peoples before Algeria became a French colony. Having acquired Algeria, it seemed logical to acquire its neighbour, Tunis. The cost and bloodthirsty wars in Algeria, however, made France hesitate, and it was only when Italy showed interest in Tunis that the French made a move. They sent 40,000 troops to Tunis and after a brief military campaign in 1881 they took control. The cost of the campaign, however, made premier Jules Ferry very unpopular with the Assembly and before long his government was brought down.

In the next two years France lost her historic links with Egypt, the most recent being Ferdinand de Lesseps' construction of the Suez Canal. Egyptian bankruptcy had compelled France and Britain to take financial control of the government in Cairo. But when an Egyptian nationalist revolt broke out and the British sent troops in, the French premier refused any part in the operation, remembering what had happened to Ferry after Tunis. He could have been less cautious, for in 1883 Ferry again became premier. A convinced imperialist, he was disgusted by the timidity which had lost France her voice in Egypt. So he encouraged colonial efforts elsewhere. A grip on Madagascar was established. Then a remarkable explorer, Savorgnau de Brazza, claimed part of the Congo basin for France. Finally, the French expanded their trading interests in Indo-China: to a foothold in Cochin China (in the south around Saigon) was added an expedition to Tonkin (in the north around Hanoi). Here French efforts became expensive; Tonkin was on China's southern frontier, and there were outbreaks of fierce fighting before French occupation was accepted. The French Assembly in Paris became increasingly agitated as Ferry asked for more money to pay for these conquests. Ferry's government was doomed once again. He was voted out in March 1885, and only just escaped from howling mobs in the streets demanding death for 'Tonkin-Ferry'.

In Africa in the 1890s the French proceeded to take their 'cut' in the scramble for territory that Britain, Germany and other European countries were engaging in. From Senegal in West Africa France established a vast Saharan empire. It was obvious that at some point European powers would clash with each other over the spoils. Costly struggles with the more powerful and independent native peoples had already been a feature of French, British and German imperialism. But at Fashoda in 1898 French and British power met head on, as French and German interests were to do in Morocco in 1905 and 1911. Captain Marchand had moved across Africa from the French Congo, to stake a claim to the upper Nile in the Sudan when he faced at Fashoda a victorious British army from Khartoum under Kitchener. Both exchanged pleasantries, refused to fight, and agreed to wait upon a London – Paris diplomatic wrangle in which Paris eventually gave way. But within six years, by the Entente of 1904, Britain and France had agreed to settle their colonial arguments. So when Germany challenged growing French influence in Morocco, Britain sided with France. By 1914, General Lyautey, the greatest of all French colonial administrators, had rounded off French control of north-west Africa.

Motives and Benefits

The story was straight forward, but explanations of who gained from imperial activities and why they were entered into were far more complex. It is clear that the foundation stones of the empire were not laid by the Third French Republican governments; the real work was done by a remarkable collection of civil servants, diplomats, explorers, soldiers and missionaries. Politicians, and then only very few of them, gave their support later, when, in many cases, a *fait accompli* had been presented to them. As the size of the empire grew it gave a valuable psychological boost to France's status as a great power. National prestige was an appealing motive to French governments. It took many years before the commercial products of her colonies made any impression on French life. The French people were uninterested or even openly hostile to some of the imperial expeditions. The Parisian press, reflecting this, regarded colonial adventures as bad for two reasons. They were too costly and they distracted attention and resources from the 'thin blue line of the Vosges', where Germany occupied France's lost provinces of Alsace and Lorraine. Dealing with Bismarck had been difficult enough, but when in the 1890s Germany was ruled by the bellicose and uncertain policies of Kaiser William II, it seemed all the more obvious that French military resources should be concentrated on her eastern borders.

Efforts by individuals to stimulate interest in colonies met with little response. Someone, as early as 1876, had pleaded in vain for France to build up 'a Mediterranean empire which will be not only a satisfaction to our pride, but certainly the last resource of our greatness'. Later, Ferry paid the price of supporting a Tunisian and Indo-Chinese empire: for wasting money on these distant places he was savagely denounced in the Assembly as 'a tool of Germany', and as we have seen, his government was defeated twice on the colonial issue.

The French Empire, then, was the creation of the men-on-the-spot. And the benefits, both for France and for the conquered, reflected the abilities, attitudes and interests of these men. Many were soldiers seeking outlets for their energies *away* from France after the defeat of 1871. Two young officers, Joffre and Galliéni, later to be famous figures in the First World War, sought their military fortunes in Timbuktu and Madagascar respectively. Galliéni's policy became widely practised throughout the empire. He called it his 'splash of oil' approach. Certain key areas would be pacified (French colonialists preferred this word to 'conquered', as it gave a better impression!), French law and administration would be firmly imposed, and then the oil-stain would spread quietly to neighbouring areas anxious for the peace and benefits of French civilisation. The likely advantages to the natives were many: peace, trade, railways, schools and hospitals. For some, too, the offer of French citizenship and partnership in the administration quickly turned important local natives into French supporters.

Progress was not always smooth. Because there was no clearly thought-out policy from Paris, colonial resources were often wasted, neglected or cruelly abused. In the French Congo, de Brazza found himself in the grip of vicious financial speculators, who used torture and mutilation of natives to force them to work at the valuable rubber trees in the forests. Elsewhere railways were built and thriving trades established – but only in goods that the French wanted; the needs of the local people were ignored. In West Africa and Indo-China alcohol and opium-dealing were lucrative to the French, but unpopular and harmful to the natives. Some of the expeditions, too, were badly organised: in the first one to Madagascar twenty men died in the fighting and 5,000 from disease. Again it became evident after some years of French rule, that French civilisation might bring hospitals, but it also brought tuberculosis and other 'white man's diseases'.

French efforts to educate their imperial subjects had unexpected results in the long term. The aim was clear, as one official put it, 'to instruct the masses and to bring out an *élite*'. It seemed an admirable one at the time, but as the empire grew bigger so the proportion of natives who won through to full partnership with the French grew smaller. The rest became, in effect, second-class citizens. In Algeria, for instance, the Arabs (mostly Moslem) could all become French citizens – on one condition, that they accepted France's Napoleonic Code of Laws. This meant, particularly, accepting the Christian rule of a man having only one wife. This meant abandoning their Islamic traditions and only a few Arabs chose to do so. Most lost all the other rights that went with citizenship, such as land ownership backed by the law courts. Within a generation Algeria became a country of two 'nations', one on top, the other below, with the majority of native Algerians working as labourers on European farms. When the Algerians demanded independence in the 1950s this gulf between the settlers and the natives proved to be a brutal, complicating factor and led to eight years of bloodthirsty civil war.

It would be wrong to end this discussion of French imperialism on a sour note. The evil that de Brazza brought to the French Congo can be sharply contrasted with what Albert Sarraut did in Indo-China. By 1914 he had removed many of the abuses of colonial rule. He refused to accept that what was right in Paris must be right everywhere. He governed the colony sympathetically, giving many more jobs to the local people, accepting the traditions of local laws, and insisting that all French officials had an expert knowledge of the many local languages. Sarraut personified Jules Ferry's vision, that France 'should carry everywhere its flag, its arms, its genius'.

6
A Portrait of French Society 1871–1914

In 1899 Jules Lemaître attempted to define *le français moyen*, his average Frenchman. 'Be he *bourgeois*, peasant or workman he is pretty much the same in all our provinces. He loves his country and the army instinctively and will not have a finger laid on them. He is genuinely imbued with the principles of 1789. Private property is one of the things he prizes most. In general he does not care much for priests, but he is not intolerant; he lets his wife and children attend Mass, but generally-speaking he avoids thinking about dogmas.'

Such generalisations concealed a rich kaleidoscope of people and opinions. Some of this variety illustrated healthy features of a civilised life, some revealed tensions and worries for the future; other aspects, especially in political divisions, exposed bitter conflict. We can get a better understanding of French society by examining in more detail some of Lemaître's features – the *bourgeoisie*, the peasantry, women and the family, the principles of 1789, for instance.

Too Few Children?

France is twice the size of Britain, and includes within her frontiers great contrasts in climate, scenery and the use of land. This diversity, accompanied by huge areas of fertile soil, had created for centuries a wealthy land for its enterprising people. Around 1900 France had 39 million inhabitants, a large number of whom could say they lived cheaply and well. There had been many improvements in diet over the past fifty years. Fine bread had always been available, but the consumption of meat had doubled, sugar and coffee trebled, and wine and potatoes were up by a half. Ninety per cent of French food was home-grown.

Trading prospects looked good. Foreign trade went up by seventy-five per cent between 1870 and 1914. France concentrated on her exports in luxury goods – silks, vintage wines, perfumes and the high fashion of women's *haute couture*. France excelled in two new and important transport fields: first, she had by far the best system of roads in Europe, and had pioneered the building of the motor-car; secondly, Blériot crossed the English Channel by aeroplane, and gave the French

Two powerful visions from past French history which influenced the attitudes of Frenchmen to the governments of the Third French Republic. Above, the Bastille prison in Paris being stormed on 14 July 1789, signalling the downfall of the ancien régime. Below, Delacroix's 1830 painting of Marianne as 'la liberté' leading revolutionary Frenchmen across the barricades

a considerable lead and prestige in European aviation.
All this seemed to point to a prosperous future. The Germans had a saying that the good life was 'to live like God in France'. Yet there were dark clouds on the horizon. One was that other countries' economies were expanding even faster. By 1900, industrialisation, in terms of machines, factories, coal and iron mining, steam-horse power, railways, business enterprise and labour skills, had become the most important factor in international power. In this respect France was simply not becoming industrialised quickly enough. A key product, for instance, was coking coal: in 1913 France produced 41 million tons, Germany 279 million tons and Britain 292 million tons. One problem was the small size of many of France's industrial undertakings – half of all her industrial workers were to be found in workshops of less than twenty people. Despite fine craftsmanship these workers gave France none of what is called economies of scale. This means that in Britain and Germany large factories could produce more things, more quickly and more cheaply.

The darkest cloud of all was that France had a declining birthrate. In 1800 France had the biggest population in western and central Europe; by 1870 that lead had gone, and by 1914 France's 39 million had to be compared with Britain's 45 million and Germany's 67 million. It caused grave concern for two reasons. First, as Germany had twice as many men as France available for conscription it put France at a disadvantage should there be a war. Secondly it stunted enterprise in the economy. The workforce was aging; the extra men needed for a big expansion were not available (a million immigrants were encouraged to come and work in France to solve this difficulty). Also, entrepreneurs, those businessmen who risk their money investing in industry, were unwilling to put much cash into greater production, for who, they argued, would buy the extra goods?

Writers disagree about the causes of this decline in the birthrate. Some suggest that large numbers of families in towns were too poor to have more than one or two children, and that widespread alcoholism reduced fertility. Others point to a high infant mortality, and to the French laws of inheritance whereby property was equally divided amongst heirs, which obviously discouraged large families. Recent research has cast doubts on some of these conclusions, even to the extent of producing opposite arguments! Professor Alfred Sauvy, a French expert on the subject, has argued that there was actually a lowering of infant mortality. This and better education meant life became a little easier, and so, as a move to the towns increased, French families were content to have fewer children – they became, Sauvy said, 'more prudent' and deliberately planned their children.

Whatever the reasons, France was being outstripped in manpower by her neighbours. The lesson was obvious: French families had too few children.

The Role of Women

French society at the end of the nineteenth century was peculiar in that a woman's status and rights inside and outside the family contrasted greatly. An Englishwoman travelling in France in 1905 declared, 'In most French households women reign with unchallenged sway'; and foreigners like Mrs Pankhurst, the English suffragette, were convinced that this was why there was no strong feminist movement. The task of bringing up children was nearly always that of the mother. The father was usually a stern, authoritarian figure in the background ('Punish the child with real severity, that is the great secret of authority', advised a parents' manual in 1890). He got away from his wife as often as possible – many husbands suspected that their wives spied on them, and told all their secrets to the priest at confession. 'It was', said one writer, 'with a mistress or at a café that the husband sang and laughed.'

Yet in many ways women were treated as inferior to men. Under French law a wife had to obey the husband, and he had the sole right to administer any property she might bring to a marriage. A Frenchwoman wrote in 1883 that there were three kinds of marriages: for love, for convenience and for duty. Yet if a woman, finding herself in the second or third kind, sought love elsewhere, she could be imprisoned for up to two years for adultery; for a man doing the same thing there was no punishment. Women were normally paid only half a man's wage, and they were banned from most professional careers. There was little opportunity for secondary or university education – the Sorbonne University in Paris refused to allow women even to attend lectures until 1880. Women were, of course, not allowed to vote, but on curious grounds. It was argued that since women went to church more often than men, giving them the vote would lend support to the clerical opponents of the Republic.

Around 1900 Frenchwomen had too many serious problems within their families to worry much about rights and status. Many children for instance did not have a full family life – for every fifteen families with both mother and father, another four had no father, and two no mother; and only half of all marriages lasted longer than fifteen years. Health was the most common worry for women. There was little knowledge of birth control and the Church forbade it; so thousands of women turned to abortion. Investigations showed that more than half a million abortions occurred each year – they were almost as normal and frequent as childbirth. Because of this women's gynaecological diseases became very common: a doctor estimated that in the towns eighty per cent of women suffered chronically from them. Amongst boys and men statistics taken from army conscription records show their poor health too. One such record revealed that of 325,000 men aged twenty, 30,000 had rickets or consumption, 16,000 were cripples or hernia sufferers, and 4,000 were completely toothless – in all, one-third were ill or deformed. There were, of course, plenty in reasonable health, and sickness was rarely serious enough for people to become bed-ridden. But it is clear that throughout France a fair proportion of women, themselves often in poor health, had to be both mother and nurse for much of their adult life.

La Bourgeoisie Française

France in the nineteenth century was dominated by the *bourgeoisie*, a middle class of people between the aristocracy on the one hand and the peasants and factory workers on the other. Around 1900 the *bourgeoisie* numbered 6 million. Its lawyers had led the Revolution of 1789, and its members had become very wealthy throughout the next century. They set the tone in dress and manners for the rest of France, and they controlled the key positions in government, industry, finance, education, the professions and the press.

If France had a ruling class before the First World War it was unquestionably the most influential and richer ones: the *haute* or *grande bourgeoisie*. Their life-style had certain characteristics. Money was important, but not just possession of it; what mattered was the way it was spent. The head of the family used it to create a distinctive style of life, one that gave a good impression of his taste to others. A particular room, the *salon*, or drawing-room in which to receive visitors, was furnished with a piano, paintings, candelabras and clocks to show a surplus of wealth which had been spent on cultured living. His wife was not allowed to work. His son had to go to a secondary school (hopefully a Parisian *lycée*) to study for the *baccalauréat;* this would take him on to a university, so that eventually he could enter a profession, and not have to work as an artisan. His daughter had to have a dowry to enable her to make a good marriage. He went to church, but visited the opera or theatre just as frequently to parade his wealth and status.

The remainder, the lesser or *petite bourgeoisie*, envied and tried to copy this life-style. But small shopkeepers, for instance, could rarely afford a *salon*. What kept the *bourgeoisie* together as a class were certain beliefs and fears, and a determination to exercise their power and influence. They believed in capitalism: in private enterprise, in competition, and in the importance of technology in ensuring mankind's progress. A *bourgeois* employer, however few his employees, regarded it as his right to 'Hire and Fire', to command others. He was the man who gave orders to others, not merely in business, but socially to his family and servants. He was the *patron,* the master of his world.

By 1900, however, he feared his orderly world was crumbling. Increasingly he was losing respect, and *'bourgeois'* was becoming a dirty word – the exploiter of the working classes. And he was genuinely frightened of the town masses, of their revolutionary force, and especially of their newly-acquired ideology, socialism. As a result the *bourgeoisie* began losing its confidence. A French politician later said, 'the sap had begun to trickle out of it', and the social and economic impact of the First World War was to shatter its comfortable world forever.

Peasants

A peasant was a countryman who owned or rented a relatively small amount of land – perhaps only one or two hectares. His life was very hard and he often lived in very poor conditions. He was fiercely independent. He wanted to be self-reliant and regarded officials with suspicion – even those who came to suggest how he might increase his crop yield. For many years his life had been one long struggle: to pay his rent, his tax, his debts (when he bought a machine or seed), and the cost of veterinary visits and stud fees. A sympathetic writer on peasant life said, 'a peasant saw the bailiff at his heels whenever a hailstorm threatened or when the frosts of May killed the fruits in flower'. But by 1900 the peasant, belonging to by far the largest group in France's 39 million people, was just beginning to feel the benefit of change. Railways were lowering the transport costs of taking his produce to town; and the French government (through the Meline Tariff of 1892) protected agricultural prices from foreign competition by imposing stiff duties on imported food. Improvements in life style too could be seen: floorboards now covered beaten earth or stone slabs, and the peasant's wooden clog-shoe, the *sabot*, was not now his only footwear.

The age-old hostility which many townsmen in France had for the peasant, however, remained the same. Some writers showed little pity for his problems. Karl Marx dismissed the peasantry as 'a sack of potatoes' – each with individual characteristics, but all the same kind. Balzac wrote a famous novel called *Les Paysans*, but he was full of contempt for them; another Parisian writer called them, 'greedy, envious, crafty, cowardly and brutal.' Emile Zola, in his novel *Earth* portrayed the peasant as a man so greedy for land that it amounted to 'an animal passion'. Most peasants made little effort to modernise. Right up to the middle of the twentieth century they remained the poorest people in France.

The vine-growing peasants illustrate the problems and attitudes of the rest of rural France very well. In the 1860s a great expansion of wine production had taken place. The peasants had always provided the wealthier classes with expensive, quality wines, but now a new market emerged with town workers wanting cheap *vin ordinaire*. This seemed to guarantee prosperity for the vine-growing peasants. Then three disastrous things happened: first, phylloxera, a vine disease, destroyed huge areas of cultivation in the south in the 1870s and 1880s; secondly, the government allowed Algeria to develop vines, and Spanish and Italian wines to be imported; thirdly, around 1900, big estate owners began mass-producing *vin ordinaire* and selling it more cheaply than the small peasant producer could. All this led to great distress, and in 1907 to some rioting. The French peasant was really a small, weak individual in a fiercely competitive world.

The 'Dangerous Class' of the Proletariat

Throughout the nineteenth century the *bourgeoisie* looked on the French factory workers as dangerous people. Meetings of workers could easily erupt into violence, which had struck terror into *bourgeois* hearts ever since the Bastille Days of 1789. As a result the government made laws to try and keep them under control. The worst of these was the *livret*, a sort of passport which the workers had to have to change jobs – without one a worker could be imprisoned as a vagabond! Though it was only partially enforced, it was clearly an effort by the ruling classes 'to maintain subordination amongst workers', as an old 1781 law put it. The French working class was perhaps the worst treated in western Europe: the *livret* was only abolished in 1890; not until 1900 did the law limit the work of women and children to a ten-hour day; only in 1906 did the labourer get a legal one day off per week (Sunday); and there were no state unemployment and sickness insurance schemes for workers such as those being tried out in Germany and Britain.

The government, however, made one concession to the workers in 1884 when it allowed them to set up trade unions, and in the late 1890s a General Confederation of Labour, the CGT, was formed. At their meetings the workers called for violence, strike action and seizure of property as the only means of winning a fair standard of living. At Amiens in 1906, the CGT proclaimed the general strike as the weapon the workers should use to overthrow the *bourgeois* government of the Third Republic; with this revolution would come control of factories by workers' syndicates or committees.

However, all this talk of revolution proved premature. The number of industrial workers in France was relatively small. From 1906 to 1914 the country was plagued with strikes, but most of them were badly organised. In 1910, when the railway unions struck, the CGT had too little money to give anything but moral support (its income was only £800 a year). The railway unions themselves were weak – only one-fifth of the 300,000 railway workers actually belonged to a union. This particular strike was easily suppressed by government intervention. The leaders were arrested and the strikers conscripted into the army.

Obviously unions need to band together if they are to have any influence on a government or on employers. The trouble with the French industrial workers was that most of them would only trust their small, local unions where they were known (there were 5,000 of these in 1912). Others were most reluctant to pay subscriptions to big federations of unions because these offered hardly any welfare benefits or strike pay. In some places, as in the mines of Carmaux, north-east of Toulouse, peasants who came looking for work kept their plots of land and never thought of themselves as full-time miners. The bulk of French workers regarded union work and attendance at meetings as a waste of time, for they had their own activities which gave them plenty of relaxation from a drab working day. In the mining community of St Etienne, near Lyon, gymnastic clubs and pigeon-breeding were very popular; in the industrial centre of Lille there were sixty-three drinking clubs, thirty-seven card clubs, twenty-three for bowls, twenty-eight for archery – all from time to time organising boisterous banquets and festivals. With such strong local loyalties and interests it is not surprising that the CGT's talk of revolution came to nothing.

A Suspicion of Income Tax and Politicians

Frenchmen were agreed on one thing: 'the best government is the one that interferes least'.[1] The novelist, Anatole France, used this argument in favour of the Third Republic: 'because it governs little, I pardon it for governing badly'. Two characteristics of French political life around 1900 were the average Frenchman's abnormal hostility to paying taxes, and his seeming unconcern at the ease and speed with which governments fell from power.

A government must have taxes to pay for keeping law and order and for defence; if it feels its colonial responsibilities are expanding or its poor need money from the state even more taxes are needed. In the past French governments had always raised the money either by borrowing it, or through taxes such as customs and payments by big landowners. Many other countries favoured income tax, because it was more dependable, and it was fairer in sharing the burden amongst rich and poor. The French, however, would have none of it. Between 1870 and 1914 many attempts to introduce income tax had been voted out by the National Assembly who argued that snooping tax-collectors would rob Frenchmen of their freedom. France entered the First World War with sixty per cent of its money coming from loans (on which, of course, the government had to pay interest). Of the rest, three-quarters came from taxes on goods bought in shops, not on income. A sour comment made at the time was that Frenchmen were willing to die for their country, but not pay for it!

Thus France presented a curious spectacle to her neighbours of a wealthy country with a poor government. Foreigners noted another oddity – her permanent political crisis. But Frenchmen rarely worried about the regular fall of their governments. They knew in their hearts that there was always the Council of State (the *Conseil d'Etat*) to be relied on. This was the most important part of the French civil service, with its corps of officials in Paris, a Supreme Court of Justice, an Inspectorate of Finances, and ninety Prefects who ran the local *départements* into which France was divided. All these men saw to it that, whatever government was in power, taxes were collected, armies raised, accounts kept, justice dispensed and civil order maintained. A French historian put it like this: 'So long as the bureaucrat is at his desk, France survives.'

[1]See the guide on page 14

The Left and the Right

The attitude of Frenchmen to politics was two-edged. As we have seen, they regarded politicians with caution or even disdain. Yet they felt passionately about political ideals, to such an extent that two rival camps had developed in the nineteenth century. Nearly every major issue of national and local life divided Frenchmen between one of two extremes, the Left and the Right. Such terms were, and are, far more meaningful to French people than party labels (the French did not have defined, disciplined political parties until the early twentieth century).

The French invented the terms Left and Right. They come from the first National Assembly created in June 1789 at the start of the great French Revolution of that year. In a big arc of seating in the Assembly building, those who supported royal power (mainly the ancient privileged estates of the nobility and clergy) sat to the right of the Speaker's chair; those who took the view that the will of the elected representatives of the people ought to prevail in any dispute sat on the left. Men who sat in the centre were uncommitted, regarding themselves as moderates. The Right stood broadly for the *status quo*, and the Left for some degree of change.

The five years following 1789 are called simply The Revolution. From then, until well into the twentieth century, the ideas of the Revolution provided the touchstone of French political opinion. The Third French Republic was broadly a government of the Left. Its supporters believed in the principles of 1789. The Revolution had swept away the privileges of the aristocracy and replaced them with new ideas: sovereignty of the people, universal male suffrage, equality before the law for all its citizens, and a passion for justice. As the Industrial Revolution developed in the nineteenth century, so the Left added other ideas to its programme: social welfare for ordinary people, Marxist demands for the nationalisation of 'the means of production, distribution and exchange', even the possible abolition of private property. Clearly the left was never a single party. Those favouring only gradual change like property owning peasants were called Radicals and were just to the left of centre; others wanting more change in favour of working-class interests were called socialists; whilst those favouring more revolutionary alterations in society were called communists, and were on the extreme left. Governments were made up of many shades of opinion, and it was possible to get only a few points of a programme accepted by the National Assembly. But the ideals were constantly re-stated, and symbolic reminders of the Revolution brought to the fore especially during election campaigns – the cry of *liberté, egalité et fraternité*, the tricolour flag, the *Marseillaise*, pictures of the storming of the Bastille by the Parisian mob, and particularly Marianne, the girl in the revolutionary cockade who, rather like St George slaying the Dragon, led Frenchmen out from the barricades against the enemies of France.

Those 'enemies' were not only foreigners but also the forces of the Right. While the Left tried to continue the work of the Revolution, the Right endeavoured to undo its results. For them the root cause of France's problems after 1870 was the wishy-washy liberal attitude of the Left. Strong, authoritarian government was needed. To achieve this the Right wanted a restoration of the monarchy; a restriction on the power of elected assemblies; an increase in the privileges and influence on public life of the aristocracy, the army and the Roman Catholic Church; and support for private or Catholic control of Schools. It was totally opposed to communism and socialism. Its watchword in economic affairs was capitalism, with its emphasis on private enterprise.

As with the Left, the Right also had its divisions of opinion. Some were merely conservative in that they resisted rapid change. Others were more reactionary and wished to return to the old privileged ways of life. A few extremists like Charles Maurras used the press to pour out their hatred for the Revolution, for democracy and the mob, for parliaments, for state education, for the Rights of Man, plus, as Maurras wrote, for the three 'alien poisoners of the Motherland – protestants, foreigners and Jews'. *La gloire* was the positive ideal of the extreme Right. Forty kings, it was said, had made France the glory of the West for a thousand years – bring them back and the glory would return.

Church and State: an Argument over Schools

One issue angered the Left more than most: the influence of the Catholic Church. Clerical power was singled out as the key danger to the Republic by Gambetta in 1877 when he declared, '*le cléricalisme, voilà l'ennemi*'. An impressive symbol of this power could be seen in Paris on the Butte of Montmartre. Sacré Coeur, the huge, white-domed church whose foundation stone was laid in 1873, dominated the skyline, and had been built from donations given by supporters of the Right. It was their penance, their way of apologising to God for the horrors of the Commune. To the Left however it was an ever-present reminder of an enemy within.

Education had long been a battlefield between the Right (who wanted the Catholic Church to keep its control over schools) and the Left (who ever since the Revolution had wanted to extend State control). In 1880 half the boys and nearly all the girls in France attended Catholic schools – partly because in most villages there was only one school and it was run by priests, monks or nuns. Jules Ferry, a determined opponent of clerical influence, put a bill through the Assembly in 1882 which made primary education free, compulsory and secular (which meant that religious supervision was banned from state schools). Ferry's other efforts to stop anybody who was not authorised by the state from teaching, and to expel powerful religious groups like the Jesuits produced such an outcry that they failed.

The Dreyfus Case made the Republican government more determined. Since the Church had given such support to the anti-Dreyfusards, it was clear that their efforts to undermine the government could be made easier by their influence in the schools. Gambetta's left-wing, anti-clerical war-cry of 1877 could be heard again. There were several thousand religious orders in France, and their 200,000 members were denounced in 1901 by the premier, Waldeck-Rousseau, as a rival

The imposing Sacré Coeur, for so long the symbol of bitterness between Right and Left in France

power within the state. He wanted to control these orders, and so passed a Law of Associations which required members of all religious groups to obtain permission for their activities from the National Assembly. Anti-clerical fervour soon went far beyond what Waldeck-Rousseau had in mind. A new premier, Emile Coombes, passionately anti-Catholic, saw to it that few permissions were granted. Coombes went on in 1904 to disestablish the Catholic Church by a Law of Separation. This meant that, though Frenchmen remained free to attend Catholic churches, the State would no longer contribute its traditional 40 million francs annually to maintain church buildings and to pay the clergy, Catholic schools would get no aid, and no religious lessons would be given in state-run schools.

There were riots as angry parents, priests and nuns tried to defy officials and police. But Coombes had won. The power of the Church in France had been effectively curbed. Soon only one-fifth of young French schoolchildren attended a Catholic school. The political cost was considerable. Instead of healing old political wounds, the Left and Right became even more antagonistic, and schools became just one more issue in the century-old struggle between the Revolution and the Counter-Revolution.

La Belle Epoque

A label has been applied to the dozen or so years either side of the turn of the century: *la belle époque*. Later generations would look back and say 'that was the time in which we'd most like to have lived'. It was seen as a period of prosperity and stability. Partly, of course, it was seeing the past through rose-coloured spectacles. Things which had made people worried or unhappy were ignored. The period was by no means *belle* for many French men and women. National concern over birthrates, family worries over ill-health, political quarrels, the long hours and hard work for low wages and little security by some factory-workers and peasants, public expression of concern that France was losing in the race for international prestige – all these ought to be taken into account when we study this period of history.

Yet people still believe that *la belle époque* must have been a fine time to live. Its image was created by the *bourgeoisie* and publicised in the great artistic achievements of the period. Visually, it is best represented in the world-wide reputation which Paris had in fashion and in the arts. Charles Frederick Worth, an Englishman with a genius for original design and a flair for elegance, set himself up in Paris, and by the 1870s had created an immense luxury industry that stood up against international fashion competition for forty years. In March 1894 *The Times* of London wrote of Worth: 'He set the taste and ordained the fashion of Paris. He knew how to dress a woman as nobody else knew how to dress her.' He introduced many features of the fashion world, which became standard in the twentieth century – mannequins to show his clothes and models not only for private customers but for sale to copy-designers in other countries. Worth's Paris Couture was much in demand by the well-to-do.

France excelled in the arts, and Paris, the City of Light, attracted poets, novelists and artists from all over the world. Her own native talent produced in a short space of time a group of painters called Impressionists. A list of their names is a roll-call of the famous – Renoir,

Haute Couture: French fashion modelled at the Longchamps Races, Paris, in 1907

Rodin's superb kneeling female, 'The Danaïde', which he sculpted from a block of marble for exhibition in 1885

Degas, Monet, Manet, Cézanne, Toulouse-Lautrec. She also excelled in other fields. Auguste Rodin produced beautiful sculpture; and Bizet, Debussy and Ravel composed world-renowned music. As well as offering high culture, Paris also presented popular entertainment. The Folies-Bergères and the Moulin Rouge music-halls were as much frequented by artists and the working classes as the Opéra and Comédie Française were by the *bourgeoisie*.

There were also important advances made in science and technology in France at this time. Pierre and Marie Curie discovered radium and made important contributions in physics and chemistry. In biology Louis Pasteur had established a universal reputation in the second half of the nineteenth century. The Pasteur Institute, opened in Paris in 1888, was dedicated to research in work he had started. He had proved that minute organisms cause disease, and had developed many kinds of vaccination, as well as originating the pasteurisation of milk. In the 1890s the Lumière brothers made the cinema a practical possibility, rather than just an inventor's toy, and a decade later Blériot was doing the same for the aeroplane and European aviation.

In 1900 a great world fair was held in Paris. It was visited by over 50 million people throughout the year. It should have been a forceful demonstration of French pride and a reminder of the glory of France; it was certainly meant to be the show-piece of the prosperous years of *la belle époque*. In the event, however, it proved rather embarrassing for France. The industrial might of France's neighbour, Germany, was put on display, and she was obviously the 'winner' in the style, range and power of her commercial exhibits. Some Frenchmen might well have wondered how long the days of wine and roses of *la belle époque* could last . . .

Part Two
France in decline 1914–47

7
'Gentlemen, we shall fight on the Marne', Joffre 1914

International Tensions

When the First World War broke out in August 1914 people were convinced that it had deep-rooted causes and had been inevitable. Plenty of explanations could be given. Germany and France had been enemies for a long time: their peoples had been at each other's throats for hundreds of years. No Frenchman could ignore the 'lost' provinces of 1871 (Alsace and Lorraine), and the press kept alive the idea that France would get them back in a war of revenge. Germany was the rising power of the age with her enormous industrial wealth, military traditions and growing navy. Her ruler, Kaiser William II, seemed happy to seize on any chance of undermining French prestige. At Algeçiras (1906) and Agadir (1911), he challenged French interests in Morocco, and tested the strength of the recent Anglo-French Entente of 1904. This Entente gradually pulled Britain and France together, although originally it had only been an agreement to settle by compromise some long-standing feuds. They had military discussions and later came to a naval agreement whereby Britain would defend French interests in the North Sea and vice versa in the Mediterranean. The French already had a military alliance with Russia (1894), each promising to support the other if attacked. These agreements, although valuable additions to French security, made the growing tension worse between the nations of Europe before 1914. Such tensions, an increasing armaments race, and the willingness of political leaders of several countries to bluff and play 'brinkmanship' to maintain prestige – all made war possible.

Yet, when a crisis occurred at Sarajevo in June 1914, involving a Serbian assassination of the heir to the Austrian imperial throne,

A political joke of 1904–5: Germany fails to part Britain and France

SOLID.

Germany. "DONNERWETTER! IT'S ROCK. I THOUGHT IT WAS GOING TO BE PAPER."

Europe's politicians still had good reason to expect a diplomatic settlement, or at worst a local Balkan struggle. What made a European conflict, with all its horrors, inevitable was not really international tension, but a combination of mobilisation procedures with the rigidity of a German military plan. When Russia ordered the mobilisation of her army to support Serbia against Germany's ally, Austria, the Germans put the Schlieffen Plan into action on 1 August 1914.

Two Plans and a 'Revolving Door'

Eight years before the crisis, the German High Command had worked out a solution to their nightmare of a war on two fronts, east and west, which could result from the Franco-Russian Alliance. Count von Schlieffen proposed that a small German force should hold a slowly mobilising Russian army in the east, whilst the main German army struck at France, defeating her in six weeks, before turning east to Russia. As speed was vital, two further points were added to the

Schlieffen Plan: to move into France via the flat plains of Belgium in a huge arc to the west of Paris; and to move according to a detailed timetable *as soon as Russia announced mobilisation* (this was the key fact which led to the 1914 conflict, as the generals demanded aggression immediately, giving the diplomats and statesmen no time to negotiate a settlement peacefully).

By 1913 the French too had completed their own ideas in Plan XVII. If war came, an all-out offensive would be launched into Lorraine and French troops would cross the Rhine; final victory would come from a north-easterly drive on Berlin. To offset the German superiority in numbers, officers in French army colleges were told to cultivate *élan* in their troops, a fighting spirit which could be transformed into a tremendous French fury which would sweep the enemy before them and win the battles. Although some officers were against this attack-at-any-cost policy, most did not take into account the changes that had been going on in weaponry – poison-gas, barbed-wire, giant guns, aircraft reconnaissance, and the machine-gun, in particular – which would give great advantages to troops defending themselves against the traditional mass attack of infantry (see map on page 52).

Both plans involved sticking to a tight timetable of mobilisation and attack. The German one was so inflexible that the commander fretted at the loss of only a few hours of 'troop movement time'. An observer on the French side described what was involved: 'Each military unit must be ready to proceed on a given day at the appointed hour to a pre-arranged destination in a train awaiting it. No change is possible during mobilisation. Improvisation when dealing with nearly 3 million men and 4,278 trains, as the French have to do, is out of the question.' The two plans have been likened to a revolving door. Neither side knew the full details of the other's plan, though they suspected a great deal. The Germans were the most hopeful: they expected the French forces would lose themselves in the wooded valleys of the upper Rhine area while their own armies moved swiftly across the plains of northern France.

The Campaign, August – September 1914

Five men dominated the execution of the plans: two Germans, von Moltke and von Kluck; and two Frenchmen, Joffre and Galliéni, aided by a small British force, the BEF, under Sir John French. None foresaw that events would be totally different from those planned.

The Germans invaded Belgium on 3 August 1914. Von Moltke had already weakened the German right wing by moving some troops hastily eastwards to face a Russian attack which had come earlier than had been anticipated. The Belgians slowed down the German advance by blowing up railway lines. The small British Expeditionary Force hurried to support Belgium (under the terms of an 1839 Neutrality Treaty) and the Germans lost further time dealing with British troops at Mons. As a result von Kluck, in command of the blunted right-wing army, whose movements were quite out of gear with what had been planned, chose not to encircle Paris from the west but to cut in to the east of the city.

Meanwhile Joffre, the French commander, had struck hard into Lorraine and what became known as the Battle of the Frontiers began. It was a costly disaster. In two weeks the French army had a third of a million casualties; the flower of their army was broken against German machine-gun fortifications, its *élan* a futile gesture.

As the Germans pressed towards the valley of the River Marne the French position looked hopeless. Then Galliéni, commander of an army to defend Paris, had information brought to him by the pilot of a reconnaissance aircraft that von Kluck's army was moving in such a way as to expose an almost undefended right flank. In the opening week of September the French generals made two decisions: Galliéni would quickly improvise an attack on von Kluck's flank, using any transport, even Paris taxis, to get troops into combat position; and Joffre would re-group his defeated armies in Lorraine and bring them rapidly to the Marne, where he also needed to persuade the BEF to stay and help. As Joffre told his senior officers, 'Gentlemen, we shall fight on the Marne.' They were fortunate decisions for the French. In four hot, dusty September days the tide of the German advance was first stopped, then turned back to the River Aisne valley. Paris was saved.

The Marne – Miracle or Muddle?

There were many verdicts on this historic battle. It seemed to some Frenchmen a miracle: Henri Bergson declared, 'Joan of Arc won the battle at the Marne.' Von Kluck commented, 'that Frenchmen who have retreated for ten days, half dead with fatigue, should be able to attack when the bugle sounds is a thing upon which we never counted'. The legend of Galliéni's 'taxicab army' grew to such proportions that Paris newspapers gave the impression that the taxis were the miraculous instrument of victory (600 cabs and buses had taken 6,000 troops on a fifty-six-kilometre journey to the front line – it was brilliant improvisation, but only that).

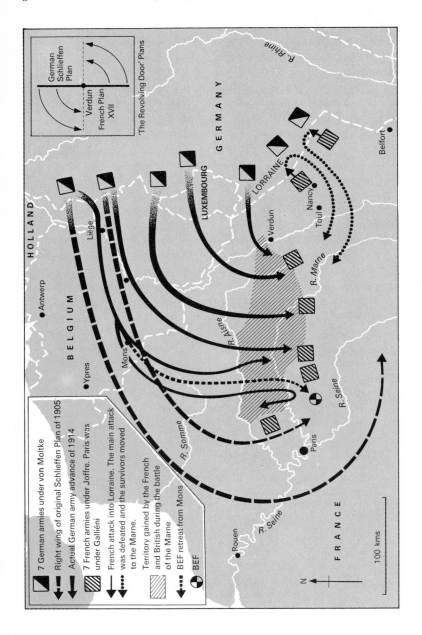

'The Revolving Door' Plans

German Schlieffen Plan

Verdun

French Plan XVII

R. Rhine

GERMANY

HOLLAND

LUXEMBOURG

LORRAINE

Belfort

Antwerp

Liège

BELGIUM

Ypres

Mons

Nancy

Toul

Verdun

R. Marne

R. Aisne

R. Somme

R. Seine

Paris

R. Seine

Rouen

FRANCE

N

100 kms

7 German armies under von Moltke

Right wing of original Schlieffen Plan of 1905

Actual German army advance of 1914

7 French armies under Joffre. Paris was under Galliéni

French attack into Lorraine. The main attack was defeated and the survivors moved to the Marne.

Territory gained by the French and British during the battle of the Marne

BEF retreat from Mons

BEF

Leadership, not a heaven-sent miracle, was the crucial ingredient of victory. Panic could well have taken hold of the French armies, as in 1870, but 'Papa' Joffre remained cool, and rapidly organised a fighting force out of the wreckage of his hopes in Lorraine. Galliéni had seen the opportunity, Joffre had forged the weapon. By contrast German decisions had meant that von Moltke and von Kluck's soldiers were already running out of steam when the French counter-attacked.

Battles rarely show plans tidily carried out, and the winners tend to exaggerate the nature and extent of their victory. The Marne was an example of both. It is worth emphasising that both French and German plans had gone wildly wrong. Just before the counter-attack Galliéni and Joffre had argued fiercely – Galliéni later suggested that the *real* battle of the Marne had been fought on the telephone! Again, there was a desperate irony in Joffre's disaster at the Battle of the Frontiers: only because he *lost* was he close enough to move quickly to the Marne for the critical battle.

There are two opposing views of the significance of the Marne. France had been saved, the Germans thrown back, and the legend of German military invincibility destroyed. This was so important that historians regard the Marne as one of the decisive battles of modern history. Others think that such a conclusion exaggerates the importance of what had happened. The retreat by the Germans to the river Aisne, pursued by the French and the BEF, had not ended because the Aisne was felt to be a good defensive position, it had ended there because it was the point where both armies became too exhausted to attack or counter-attack any more. Both sides began to dig in, and eventually a line of trenches stretched from the Channel coast to the Swiss border. The Marne was decisive, but not in the usual sense of winning a war. What it decided was that two roughly equal sides should slog it out for four murderous years; across the trenches each launched monstrous offensives in which tens of thousands were killed to gain mere yards, and to exchange one wet-bottomed trench for another.

One such battle in 1916 scarred French minds for generations: Verdun.

Opposite: *1914 – the German Schlieffen Plan in theory and practice, and the Marne campaign*

8
Verdun to Versailles

Stalemate

Even well-informed military men in 1914 expected the war to be 'over by Christmas'. But because the trenches were defensive lines and difficult to capture, little progress was being made by either side. There were many offensives throughout 1915 but, mainly because of the machine guns and barbed wire, neither side broke through the enemy lines. Commanders on both sides could see only two possibilities of breaking the stalemate: bigger guns (which could pound the enemy before an attack), and more men (which at a given point of attack would give a numerical superiority of at least five, and ideally ten, to one). Giant pieces of artillery and millions of men – both were drawn like iron filings to a magnet in February 1916. That magnet was Verdun, the famous fortress close to France's frontier and guardian of the route to Paris. Here the Germans, under their new commander Falkenhayn, were determined to break through and 'bleed France white' if necessary. The French on the other hand were determined that the Germans would be held – *'ils ne passeront pas'* became the watchword.

A remarkable testament to the courage and patriotism of the ordinary French soldier – the *poilu* – was that he could put up with the horrors of trench life. The worst horror was the constant shelling: exploding shells broke into whirling fragments that easily mutilated human bodies. A fine French novel of the war, Barbusse's *Le Feu*, described how men were 'squashed, cut in two, divided from top to bottom, blown into showers by an ordinary shell, bellies turned inside out, skulls forced into the chest as if by a blow with a club'.

Facing up to such hideous possibilities, month after month, as the war seemed to stretch out indefinitely was bad enough, but the *poilu's* normal life too, in and out of the front line, was most uncomfortable. French officers had little personal contact with the men and hardly bothered themselves with the *poilu's* welfare. Pay was very low, and in rest camps, kitchen, bath and lavatory provisions were badly neglected. When he moved up to the front line trenches the *poilu* had to carry about forty kilogrammes of equipment (including blankets, coats, shovels, eating utensils, four days rations, 200 cartridges, six hand-grenades and a gas mask) as he slithered over the mud and rubble churned up by the incessant shelling. Once there he had to submit to iron discipline. Failure to obey any orders could result in a swift court martial and execution within twenty-four hours. If a regiment failed badly in combat, men were selected at random from each unit and shot – the reason for this being '*pour encourager les autres*'. In the gaps between attacks boredom was the greatest difficulty – there was nothing to do but sit in trenches often up to the ankles in water, rarely free from evil-smelling mud and lice, and having to live with large rats that scurried about.

The Attack at Verdun

Battles are normally measured in hours or at most in days. Verdun was different. It must be measured in months. It began on 21 February 1916; the worst of the fighting took six months; and it was to be ten months before both sides finally recognised that no decision would come on that battlefield. The German effort was gigantic. For the opening day they brought up over a thousand heavy guns to bombard a front of only twelve kilometres. The biggest of them, the 'Big Berthas', fired a shell which was forty-three centimetres in diameter, was as high as a man and weighed a tonne; when fired the concussion smashed windows three kilometres around. In all the Germans kept up a round-the-clock bombardment for six days, showering $2\frac{1}{2}$ *million* shells on Verdun. Then they attacked. Within three days French morale began to crumble. One general found he had lost one-third of his 12,000 men in thirty-six hours. Roads became impassable – an ambulance took ten hours to cover thirty kilometres in the second week. The French Army Command had to act quickly or retreat. They decided to send General Pétain, an organising genius of a man, to take command. Determined to fight on, Pétain needed supplies for counter-attacking. So he ordered that the road running south out of Verdun, the 'Sacred Way' as it came to be called, must be kept open. Along it 3,000 lorries were to pass day in, day out for six months. Incredible statistics built up. The distance these lorries eventually travelled was calculated at twenty-five times around the Earth's equator. In the first week alone, 25,000 tonnes of supplies were brought in. Over the six months the French poured seventy-eight army divisions (a division was about 12,000 men) into the mincing machine of Verdun. An American observer watching the dimly-lit vehicles on the Sacred Way thought they resembled 'the folds of some

A cartoon which tried to raise French and British morale in the dark days of 1916. A small victory on the Somme front is acclaimed, but by the end of the year the stalemate seemed just as unbreakable

COMRADES IN VICTORY.
Combles, September 26th.
Poilu. "BRAVO, MON VIEUX!"
Tommy. "SAME TO YOU, MATE."

gigantic and luminous serpent which never stopped and never ended'.

The French line held. By March it was the Germans' turn to count the losses; one senior officer described the spectacle of wounded men streaming back past his HQ as being 'like a vision of hell'. By June each side had lost over a quarter of a million men, killed or wounded. Final losses were difficult to establish: after the war some 150,000 unidentified, unburied fragments of corpses were collected and placed in one vast grave.

Who won? A German who was there, Prince Max von Baden, wrote in his memoirs that Verdun 'ended in bitter disillusionment all round. We and our enemies shed our best blood in streams, and neither we nor they had come one step nearer victory.' Historians writing long after the event agree with this. Alistair Horne, in his book on Verdun called *The Price of Glory*, concludes: 'Neither side "won" at Verdun. It was the indecisive battle in an indecisive war.'

Aftermath: Mutiny, 1917

Late in April 1917 a disturbing incident occurred. Behind the French army lines near Soissons, soldiers of an infantry regiment refused to move into battle. Leaflets bearing the words, 'Death to the warmongers' were circulated. It was a short-lived incident, but it proved to be an early symptom of the biggest mutiny the French army has ever known.

By May discontent was spreading like a forest fire. In one critical week groups of men from fifty-four divisions (nearly half the entire French army) were either deserting, demonstrating or disobeying orders. Some seized trains and set off for Paris to bring their grievances before the government. Others, bewildered by the confusion around them, made themselves incapably drunk with cheap red wine. At least 20,000 deserted in May. The French commander-in-chief, Nivelle, was dismissed and replaced by Pétain, the hero of Verdun. But the first weeks of June were critical. Army leaders made frantic efforts to restore morale. Pétain combined ruthlessness in punishing ring-leaders with a genuine concern for the welfare of the troops. 'Mutineers,' he later wrote, 'drunk with slogans and alcohol, must be forced back to their obedience.' He visited ninety divisions and convinced the men that they were no longer going to be regarded as cannon-fodder. He organised immediate improvements in leave arrangement: *poilus* were no longer to travel in cattle trucks which often stayed in railway sidings for hours whilst war materials went by. Rations were improved and proper three-day rest periods were guaranteed. Pétain promised that there would be no more costly offensives. His new plan was to hold the line and wait for the arrival of the Americans, who had entered the war against Germany in April 1917. Pétain proved to be the man for the job; the mutineers were silenced.

How serious were the mutinies? No one, even to this day, has ever given a full answer to this question. What is known is that the mutinies were *behind* the front line. At no time did the French soldiers refuse to defend the trenches immediately facing the enemy. Incredibly, the Germans knew little of the mutinies. General Ludendorff said in his memoirs, that 'only vague information gradually came to our notice'. It was a grim fact that the fate of France hung on a thread. If the Germans had launched a big attack in the Aisne valley sector, where the mutinies were concentrated, it is hard to see how the allies could have stopped the enemy reaching Paris. It was not only the Germans who were ignorant of the real situation. By an extraordinary feat of French censorship practically nothing was known by most civilian Frenchmen, by the British government, and even by the British Commander-in-Chief, Field-Marshal Haig, until Pétain told him on 7 June. These clouds of secrecy lasted a long time, and years later historians had difficulty in uncovering the whole truth. 'Mutiny', for instance, is a strong, emotional word, and few armies care to keep, let alone publish, full details of what happened. The French official war history refused to use the word; instead it was called 'collective indiscipline'.

There was some doubt too about the most important reasons for the mutinies. The immediate causes were obvious: war-weariness after nearly three years of battle strain, lack of rest, the incessant noise of the guns, and the huge casualties at Verdun and elsewhere; poor pay and inadequate leave merely made matters worse. But two other causes, in Pétain's view, turned a very difficult situation into a near-catastrophe. 1917 was the year of the Russian Revolution and 16,000 Russians were fighting in France as part of the allied effort. These men became restless and mutinous as news of the disintegration of the Czar's regime in Russia filtered through. In turn they infected the French *poilu*. But Pétain's real worry was the anti-war propaganda that built up to the rear of the trenches. At the Paris railway stations anti-war leaflets were handed out to soldiers on leave-trains. Munition-workers in the factories, embittered by the shortages, the huge casualties and the lack of victories went on strike (there were 170 strikes in June 1917 alone). Pétain wrote angrily to the political authorities in the capital, 'The incitement is coming from the rear. There is an organisation at work in which the enemy has a hand.'

It is also difficult to decide how ruthless the military commanders were in dealing with mutineers. After official trials, 412 were sentenced to death though only 55 of these were actually executed. But we can only guess how many more were shot without the fuss of a trial.

Clemenceau, Foch and Victory

The whole war between the Battle of the Marne in 1914 and the spring of 1918 consisted for the French, of hundreds of small or big 'Verduns'. The British played their part in senseless frontal attacks at Ypres in 1915 and 1917, and at the Somme in July 1916. The first *day* of the Battle of the Somme, meant to relieve pressure on Verdun, cost 58,000 dead or wounded. This, the greatest disaster in the whole of British military history, went on like Verdun for week after week. It merely maintained the stalemate. Final German defeat in 1918 was due to several factors: exhaustion, shortages, rioting and naval mutinies inside Germany; a calculated but disastrous decision by Germany to torpedo even neutral ships trading with Germany's enemies (which brought the USA in to the war); and defeat on the battlefields of northern France.

But it proved a close thing for France. War-weariness and anti-war propaganda behind the French battle lines had grown worse. Clemenceau, the controversial iron man of French journalism and politics, though seventy-six years old, was summoned to be premier in November 1917. He tried to create a 'will to victory', and ruthlessly dismissed from government any waverers. He was not popular, but his war dictatorship was vitally needed when the military situation got worse. After the Bolsheviks seized power in Russia they made peace with Germany. This meant that relatively fresh German troops were able to move from the eastern front to France, and under their commander, Ludendorff, they smashed through the trench positions in March 1918. Only the steady arrival of American soldiers and equipment, and the support Clemenceau gave to the appointment of General Foch to a new post, overall commander of the allied forces, prevented total collapse. Foch made an interesting contribution. In face of all previous German attacks, generals had rushed reserves in to fill any local breach – the line, it was felt, must be preserved. Foch, though heavily criticised at the time, allowed the German onslaught to move from the line of trenches on the Aisne to the Marne. Here, Foch argued, a war of movement would again be possible, and only then did he throw in his powerful American-reinforced reserves. This time the Second Battle of the Marne was decisive, although it took another six months of bloody fighting before the Germans agreed to an armistice in November 1918.

Clemenceau worked hard at the peace conference. He constantly stressed France's need for security. He succeeded in reducing German power: her eastern frontiers were much curtailed, Alsace and Lorraine were returned to France, and a demilitarised zone along the Rhine seemed to safeguard his country against sudden attack. Further, reparations – the 'bill' for the war – were to be paid, so that France could rebuild her battle-scarred north-eastern lands. French pride was restored, but Clemenceau failed to get a crucial guarantee of French security from the USA and Britain.

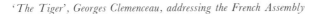

'The Tiger', Georges Clemenceau, *addressing the French Assembly*

9
The 'Twenties

Illusions

France had won, the Treaty of Versailles was signed, and a magnificent Victory Parade took place on Bastille Day, 14 July 1919. It was a great spectacle. Joffre and Foch were there, the man who had saved France in 1914 on the Marne riding beside the architect of victory in 1918. They were followed by soldiers representing all France's allies from the Americans and the British to the Italians and the Serbs. At the end a huge French contingent took an hour to pass the Arc de Triomphe. Afterwards Parisians danced through the streets of their city turning it, wrote an English newspaper correspondent, into 'one vast ballroom'.

On that day the cost of the war in human terms was forgotten by most people. But, as one foreigner, Winston Churchill, later warned, 'Victory was to be bought so dear as to be almost indistinguishable from defeat.' To a few thoughtful Frenchmen a sombre note was struck in the Victory Parade. Preceding Joffre and Foch, representing as they did *la gloire*, came the *mutilés*, those crippled by the war. The blind were led by the one-legged or armless; others had destroyed faces hidden behind bandages; the skin of many was still tinted green from the effects of chlorine gas. They represented the 740,000 hopelessly maimed soldiers in hospitals all over France. They were there too to represent France's lost legions – the 1,300,000 men who had been killed (twenty-seven per cent of all French males between the ages of eighteen and twenty-seven).

Haunted by these appalling casualties France nevertheless had considerable faith in the immediate future. For some time after the war France held certain beliefs about her victory which were not really true. She believed, for instance, that having won the war with Britain and the USA, these allies would never abandon her. Frenchmen also believed that their own army would be able to enforce the peace and that the cost of the war would be borne by the Germans. This last one was a simple belief that neatly solved two problems – that the Germans would help in the French recovery, and that such payments would prevent Germany from ever again being a military menace.

One by one each belief proved naïve or unfounded. Clemenceau recognised this when he entitled his memoirs, *The Grandeur and Misery of Victory*. Late in 1919 the first hope faded. President Wilson of the USA, whose League of Nations idea promised the peace and support France wanted, failed to get the American politicians in Congress to accept it. Britain, too, gradually drifted away from her war-time ally. She had her own domestic difficulties, and several Englishmen expressed feelings that Clemenceau had treated Germany too harshly at the Versailles peace negotiations of 1919.

So France had to face the problems of economic recovery with little support from America or Britain. First she counted the cost, then looked to Germany to pay up.

Reparations, the Ruhr and Financial Disaster

The French people's hope that Germany could and would pay the reparations was soon to be dashed. Nothing could repay the human cost, but in material terms France had paid out a quarter of her gold reserves, her 'national fortune' one might say; and seven per cent of her land had been devastated, concentrated mostly in the rich industrial regions of the north-east. The statistics made disturbing reading: $3\frac{1}{4}$ million hectares of fertile soil (or nearly the size of Holland) had been blasted; 5,600 kilometres of rails and 48,000 kilometres of roads were ruined; flooded mines reduced France's coal output to a third of her 1914 production; and hundreds of thousands of homes and factories had been destroyed. On top of this, France owed money to her allies.

When these costs were worked out, the reparations, as they were called, came to 134,000 million gold francs. This was an enormous figure, especially when compared with the 5,000 million which Germany had imposed on France back in 1871, but France justified it on the grounds that it would help pay off her own national debt. There are two main ways any government can pay for a war and reconstruction afterwards: by heavy taxation of people's incomes, or by borrowing from its own citizens and from abroad. The French governments during the war had adopted the second method and, in the expectation of reparations, continued the policy afterwards. So the debt mounted to astronomical proportions.

In presenting their 'bill' to the treaty-makers of 1919 the French not only included the 134,000 million gold francs worth of goods and property, but they *increased* the account to well over 200,000 million to include pensions for the widows and disabled for many years to come. The whole vexed question of how much was owed to whom became so

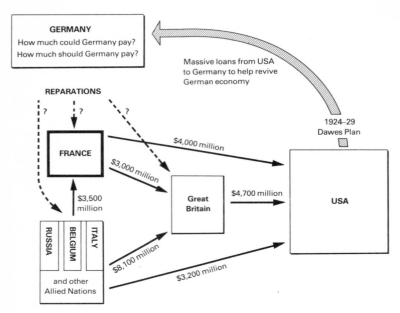

GERMANY
How much could Germany pay?
How much should Germany pay?

Massive loans from USA
to Germany to help revive
German economy

REPARATIONS

FRANCE

$4,000 million

$3,000 million

1924–29
Dawes Plan

$3,500 million

Great Britain

$4,700 million

USA

RUSSIA   BELGIUM   ITALY

and other Allied Nations

$8,100 million

$3,200 million

Start with France and follow her debts – given in figures
rounded off to the nearest 100 million, and converted to
US dollars. Then note (1) where France expected
repayments of *her* loans to come from (yet Soviet
Russia refused to honour Czarist debts, so the biggest
slice of 'Other allied nations' debts' proved impossible
to recover); and (2) French reliance on reparations from
Germany – her 'bill' to the Reparations Commission
included not only those war debts but internal damage
and costs *and* future pensions to war-widows, etc.

The Reparations Tangle

difficult that the peacemakers refused to settle a final figure for France
or any other country. Germany would begin paying in cash and
material goods, but as Lloyd George said, 'to fix a definite sum was like
asking a man in the maelstrom of the Niagara Falls to fix the price of a
horse', and he regarded the French sum as outrageous. A special
Reparations Commission was set up to sort it out by 1921, when
Germany was expected to agree to settle the account in instalments over
thirty years. Things began to go wrong from the start. It soon became a
question, not of how much Germany *should* pay, but how much she *could*
pay. Such a figure was, of course, a matter of guesswork not proper
economic accounting, and the Germans took advantage of the
uncertainty. They asked for time to pay even the early instalments.

French patience rapidly wore thin, and they became unreasonably awkward.

A payment of timber from Germany failed to arrive. Premier Poincaré decided on tough action. On 11 January 1923 French troops were ordered into the Ruhr, the industrial heart of Germany, producing three-quarters of her coal and steel. Belgian troops went in too, but Britain disapproved of such drastic action over what she regarded as a technical error. The German reaction could hardly have been foreseen by the French. The German government encouraged the Ruhr workers to go on strike and paid them out of public money – hurriedly printing notes that quickly became worthless. Faced with a general strike the French sent in their own technicians to keep the railways, mines and steel plants working. It was costly, but temporarily it seemed to work. By September the German government gave in and hoping for some American aid, agreed to resume reparations. The 'victory' proved empty. Poincaré horrified some of his political colleagues, including President Millerand and Marshal Foch, by 'bungling an opportunity'. Instead of putting pressure on the Germans to hand over the Ruhr to joint Franco-German management (with France in real control), Poincaré rather lamely agreed to submit the whole reparations question to a new international committee headed by an American, General Charles Dawes. This resulted in the Dawes Plan which reduced the reparations bill, and actually agreed that America should lend Germany money to help pay the bill and to get her industries restarted. For Germany it worked, and she enjoyed five years of relative prosperity. For France the dreadful reality dawned: she would receive only a trickle of the expected payments. (France actually received in the 1920s only four per cent of the figure agreed to by the 1921 Commission, which was itself much less than the French claim.) Poincaré became known as 'Poincaruhr', and was defeated in the May 1924 election.

The most important question in France now was whether the government would be able to repay all its loans. The anxiety of the French moneyed classes and foreign bankers produced a new difficulty called 'the battle for the franc'. In general economic terms countries need a currency that is stable (i.e., respected by its own citizens and foreigners as being a worthwhile medium of exchange for goods and services). In France the fear spread that the franc would collapse and lose its value and that the government would be forced to print more and more paper francs to pay its creditors. By 1926 the 'battle' reached a crisis. There were demonstrations in Paris. The government dithered and cabinets broke up – one only lasted a few hours. The increase in the number of extra francs required to buy, say, a pound's worth of British goods can be seen from the following table:

francs for £1

1918	26	1924	120
1919	51	1925	130
1922	73	May 1926	178
1923	85	July 1926	240

Terrifying as this inflation must have seemed at the time, things were not as bad as the figures suggested. A stable French currency required three things: that people had confidence in it and in the government, that there were plenty of jobs, and that the country should not have to rely on foreign 'gifts' (e.g. reparations) to restore the franc to pre-war levels. Surprisingly, Poincaré was the man the French turned to. After two years of incompetent governments they saw in him perhaps a

The French industrial boom 1927–31: the car firm, Citroën, using American assembly-line methods of manufacture to produce for the mass market

The 'fashion' in French car salesmanship in 1925

sensible man who meant business. He increased taxation and people saw immediately that inflation was not going to get worse. Confidence returned, and almost as a bonus it was realised that French industry was recovering faster than anyone dared hope.

An Industrial and Cultural Boom

Whilst the franc had occupied the thoughts of politicians and the headlines of the newspapers, a quiet revolution was taking place in some of France's industries. The government granted funds to rebuild factories in the devastated areas, and the recovery of Alsace and Lorraine, with their steel mills and rich iron ore and potassium deposits, was a great boost to the reconstruction programme. Certain industries –

motor vehicle, electrical, aviation, rubber and chemical – grew considerably. These were the new twentieth-century industries using advanced technology and organised on a big scale. At last France's slow industrialisation of the late nineteenth century might 'take-off' and sustain its growth, as had happened in Britain, Germany and USA.

In motor-car production, for instance, firms like Renault and Peugeot had already made their name for quality vehicles before 1914. Now in the 'twenties André Citroën put some of his great wealth, made from wartime armaments, into mass production of inexpensive cars. Citroën copied American assembly-line methods and launched vast advertising campaigns. He even advertised his cars with illuminated signs on the Eiffel Tower, which some Parisians considered in vulgar taste. Sales increased as the *bourgeoisie* showed their eagerness to own motor vehicles. Michelin, too, began its highly successful specialist tyre production. The result: France in 1929 led European car production with 245,000 vehicles that year.

These developments were accompanied by a rise in living standards assessed by one historian at over thirty-three per cent over the decade. The French regarded Britain with some disdain in 1926 – in contrast to the millions out of work there, where it was the year of the General Strike, France had a mere 585 unemployed who sought help from the government. The five years before 1931 were remembered by Frenchmen and overseas visitors alike as one of the happiest times of the Third Republic. The newspapers were full of patriotic exploits. In tennis Suzanne Lenglen's individual brilliance and the national team's victory in the Davis Cup were celebrated; and France's traditional standing in aviation was enhanced by the long-distance achievements of Saint-Exupéry.

Paris was once again the cultural capital of the world. An American journalist wrote as one of the many students, writers, painters, designers and tourists who were 'attracted by the "City of Light" with its beauty, charm, civilities, its balmy air of freedom, its appreciation of the arts'. On the Left Bank of the River Seine there was a foreign literary 'colony' led by Ernest Hemingway and Scott Fitzgerald from America and James Joyce from Ireland. France had its own native literary figures to be proud of, like Marcel Proust; and one man, Jean Cocteau, gave his great and varied talents to writing, painting, ballet, music, the theatre and the cinema. Jules Romain described Paris in the late 'twenties as 'a place and a time without equal in the history of the world'. The tragedies of the First World War and the disappointments of the immediate post-war years were best forgotten.

10
The 'Thirties: a Dismal Record

'Perhaps God is a Frenchman after all'

In 1929 most Frenchmen had confidence in the future. The 1914–18 war
was slowly passing into memory; France was economically prosperous;
politically, Poincaré had brought stability to French government; and
beyond her borders international agreements to end war, secure frontiers
and limit armaments promised peace for the foreseeable future. Even that
mattered little to some Frenchmen because plans were afoot for an
impregnable line of fortifications along the German frontier. It was
begun in 1930 and called the Maginot Line.

Even when that great world economic crisis known as the 'Depression'
or the 'Slump' began in the USA in October 1929, France was unaffected
throughout 1930 and most of 1931. Neither the rising unemployment in
advanced industrial countries, nor even the election of 107 Nazi Party
members to the German Reichstag in 1930 seemed to worry Frenchmen.
An English journalist visiting France in the following year, remarked,
'Perhaps God is a Frenchman after all.'

How Things Went Wrong

The Depression struck France late in 1931. The causes were complicated. It certainly began in the USA in the late 'twenties when
farmers produced too much food and found it difficult to sell; this meant
that the farmers became poorer and were unable to buy industrial goods
which in turn led to a slump in industry. This slump came at the same
time as millions of people were investing their money in the stock
exchanges of America and Europe, confidently expecting good rates of
interest. When these people realised goods were not being bought
at the rate they had expected they rushed to sell their shares before
their value went down. This led to the 'Wall Street Crash' in New York
in October 1929 (Wall Street being the centre of the American stock
exchange). This sequence of events hit other countries with export
industries because the USA stopped buying foreign goods. France,
which grew most of her own food, was not so dependent on exports;
she hoped the Depression would pass her by. But confidence waned,

and when Britain devalued her pound in 1931 (this meant her goods became cheaper for foreigners to buy and so fewer people would buy the more expensive French goods) French investors rushed to sell their French shares on the Bourse, the Paris Stock Exchange. French production fell, and in 1932 unemployment rose to five times the 1931 figure.

The Depression was never as bad in France as it was in Britain and Germany, but as the numbers applying for state financial help rose to nearly half a million the French government looked for economies. Defence costs in particular were cut – yet a few Frenchmen noticed that the cuts were taking place in the same period as Germany walked out of the World Disarmament Conference, and Hitler, in January 1933, became Chancellor. Some of the views of Hitler and the Nazi Party were well known. The Nazis were passionate German nationalists and had a hysterical hatred of the Jews and democracy. Hitler himself was a powerful orator and an able, if unscrupulous, politician. It was against a background of Hitler's ruthless and aggressive policies that thoughtful Frenchmen went uneasily about their daily lives in the 1930s.

Other Frenchmen were more concerned with the renewed instability of their own government. Since Poincaré's three-year period of office many presidents and premiers had tried to repeat his stability without success. The French electoral system allowed many shades of opinion to be represented, so, as always in a crisis, there was little chance of loosely-formed parties staying together. The consequences were fatal. The historian, Alfred Cobban, has written, 'The repeated slaughter of cabinets provided an opportunity for communists and fascists to concentrate their fire on the incompetence and corruption of republican politics.' Ghosts of the previous scandals and crises – *seize mai*, Boulanger, Panama and Dreyfus – stalked the land.

Stavisky

On the morning of 30 December 1933 newspapers revealed that a warrant had been issued for the arrest of Serge-Alexandre Stavisky for fraud. He was a clever, lucky swindler who had for some years been cultivating friends in important government positions. He had, for instance, obtained a letter from the French Minister of Labour supporting a 200 million franc investment in a big municipal pawnshop in Bayonne in south-west France; Stavisky had backed the scheme himself with what he claimed was some extremely valuable jewellery. This proved to be fake: hence the warrant. Further press investigations uncovered a murky world of government and police corruption.

Stavisky, it was shown, had been in trouble with the police since the mid-'twenties; arrested then, he had been released on bail whilst his complicated swindles were unravelled for his trial. But Stavisky had friends in the Assembly and in the Justice Department: he had never come to trial. Over seven years it was 'postponed' nineteen times, during which period he still found money to buy two newspaper companies, a Paris theatre and a stable of race-horses! Forty-five different complaints had been made against him concerning various frauds, but nothing was ever done about them. With the Bayonne affair however Stavisky had practised one deception too many. The press probed further. Two men were named as being chiefly responsible for the nineteen postponements of Stavisky's trial. One, Chief Prosecutor Pressard, was the brother-in-law of the French premier; the other, Albert Prince, was the assistant prosecutor – he was later found dead on the Paris-Dijon railway line, drugged and tied to a rail. Meanwhile Stavisky had disappeared. He was traced to a French alpine resort. On 8 January 1934 newspapers announced that Stavisky had committed suicide just as the police were breaking into his chalet. By now the stink of 'corruption in high places' was so great that few Frenchmen believed this; they were sure he had been murdered to prevent him from revealing how many police and government friends had benefited from his frauds. A year later a special investigation discovered the truth: Stavisky had in fact shot himself but had only succeeded in making a serious wound; the police had refused to help him for more than an hour whilst he slowly bled to death. Long before this last investigation, however, the Stavisky Affair had brought France to the brink of civil war.

6 February 1934: the Battle in the Place de la Concorde

There were many groups in France who hated the Third Republic and its parliamentary processes. Of these groups, or Leagues as they were called, the oldest was Maurras' *Action Française*, whose right-wing sympathies had gained much publicity in the Dreyfus Affair of the 1890s. There were several new Leagues, the largest being the *Croix de Feu* – its members mainly ex-servicemen, its leader a retired colonel, de la Rocque. Their programmes were very similar. The ideas of 1789, of *liberté, egalité, fraternité* were rejected, as was democracy, which Maurras declared 'took away power from the élite and gave it to the herd'. The sympathies of the Leagues were with the Fascist and Nazi parties in Italy and Germany, especially in their emphasis on strong leadership, the totalitarian power of the state, and hatred of Jews. These Leagues received their main support in Paris, and could rely on many right-wing journalists to publish their speeches. The Stavisky scandal was a sensational opportunity. Certain Paris newspapers printed hysterical appeals to the people to rise up against parliament and the government and 'chase the robbers' from the Chamber of Deputies.

On the evening of 6 February 1934 several thousand members of the Leagues converged on the Place de la Concorde, the great square just across the Seine from the Chamber. Their demonstration was met by mounted charges of steel-helmeted guards. The crowds replied with stones, iron-bars and fireworks; marbles and razor-blades on the ends of sticks were terrible weapons against the horses. As they slowly forced the police across the bridge towards the Chamber, firing broke out. For the next six hours the street fighting grew uglier. High pressure water hoses just kept the 10,000 leaguers at bay. Inside the Chamber order disintegrated. The Right kept shouting 'Resign' to the government; above the din some groups could be heard singing the *Marseillaise;* the

6 February 1934–crowds and mounted police clash in the Place de la Concorde

socialist and communist Left countered with cries of 'Power to the Soviets' and sang the *Internationale*. As the turmoil grew, members tried to slip away quietly. By mid evening the Chamber was empty, but the government and its more moderate supporters had stood firm, and at one point had gained a vote of confidence. There was a critical moment outside the Chamber just before midnight. De la Rocque had had the chance to bring up more support, but he had hesitated too long. A determined charge by the *gendarmerie*, by now reinforced and well-led, cleared the rioters from the bridge and from the Place de la Concorde.

In retrospect there is little doubt that had the leaguers been more united, and had Colonel de la Rocque of the formidable *Croix de Feu* been less cautious, French parliamentary procedures could have been destroyed. Even de la Rocque's enemies later admitted that he had the opportunity in his grasp but muffed it. A chronicler of these events has concluded that on 6 February 1934, 'a projected revolution went off at half-cock'. It had been the bloodiest street-fighting in Paris since the days of the Commune.

Léon Blum's Front Populaire

The three political parties of the Left – the Radicals, the Socialists and the Communists were horrified by the events of 1934. It was obvious that they ought to form a united front against the Right, yet their own rivalries were long-standing and not easily buried.

Slowly, the Left overcame its internal suspicions. The Soviet Communist Party in Moscow eased the problem by publishing in its newspaper, *Pravda*, a plea for the French Left to cooperate against the fascist dangers of Nazi Germany. So, on Bastille Day 1935, a third of a million communists, socialists and radicals marched together in a Paris demonstration. They needed to prove to the ordinary people of France that they could present massive support for the Third Republic, despite its shortcomings. The Socialist leader Léon Blum became the architect of a united party of the Left, the *Front Populaire*. In his programme he denounced the Leagues and vigorously attacked the *haute bourgeoisie* – singling out for special mention the 'two hundred families', the richest in France, who, through the Bank of France, were suspected of exercising enormous power behind the scenes of government. He used the slogan 'Bread, Peace and Liberty' to appeal to the voters, and said that security against Hitler would be guaranteed by a Franco-Soviet Russian alliance. On a Sunday in April 1936, despite the wet weather which usually discouraged voters, there was a huge turn-out of electorate. The *Front Populaire* emerged victorious with at least 380 supporters in the French Assembly against 230 for the parties of the Right.

The well-to-do *bourgeoisie* and aristocratic families of France viewed this turn of events as menacing. They were convinced their privileges and property were at risk and that France was on the verge of a red revolution. These fears were not entirely baseless. A spontaneous outburst of strikes in different parts of the country, in which the workers 'occupied' the factories, brought industrial production to a standstill. Blum, under pressure from all sides, called a meeting of employers and trade unionists at his official residence in Paris, the Hôtel Matignon, and won considerable concessions from the employers: a rise in wages of about twelve per cent, holidays with pay, and the promise of a forty-hour working week. The Matignon Agreement of 1936 was a political triumph for Blum. He had halted the strike movement which looked like taking the law into its own hands, and the workers thought they had made great gains. Tragically, Blum had little understanding of economics. The reforms had to be paid for, yet the forty-hour week merely *reduced* French production, and thus her total wealth; at the same

The 1936 Election: communist and other left-wing supporters on a demonstration march near the Billancourt Renault car works

time the *bourgeoisie* remained alarmed, and proceeded to convert their francs into gold or 'safer' foreign currencies. So Blum's government had to deal with a similar financial crisis to that of a decade ago.

Yet it was events abroad which set the seal on Blum's fate. In March 1936 Hitler had sent his troops into the Rhineland, which since the signing of the Versailles Peace Treaty of 1919 had been 'demilitarised'. The French took no action. Hitler had succeeded in a gamble. He said later, 'If the French had marched against us in the Rhineland, we would have had to withdraw with our tails between our legs, for our military resources would have been totally inadequate.' (Subsequently, people realised that March 1936 was a moment of destiny: the Rhineland affair was the last real chance of stopping Hitler.) The Spanish Civil War also began in 1936, but Blum's government refused to become involved. Feelings of moral guilt welled up among the French Left after their failure to aid the Spanish Republican Government in its vain efforts to resist General Franco's right-wing dictatorship. Blum's government died a lingering death early in 1937.

Why Frenchmen Prefer to Forget the 'Thirties

1938 was the year Hitler moved into Austria, and later demanded monstrous concessions for the German-speaking peoples in that part of Czechoslovakia called the Sudetenland. The French premier who came to power in April of that year was Edouard Daladier. He tried to put on a brave face, calling his government one of National Defence. But he and his party, the Radicals, recoiled in horror at the thought that another world war might break out. At Munich, in September, Daladier joined Neville Chamberlain of Great Britain in 'appeasing' Hitler and they allowed large and valuable parts of Czechoslovakia, a state France had agreed to help protect, to be given over to Nazi rule. But all that Britain and France had done was to purchase a postponement of war.

On taking office Daladier complained that France was viewed abroad as 'a drab country frightened about her future'. How true was this? In view of what happened in 1940 it is worth pausing a moment to analyse what had gone wrong. Four points can be made:

1 Military complacency

The Maginot Line had been completed in 1935. It ran from the Swiss border to Longwy, close to the southern tip of the Belgian frontier, and was an impressive engineering feat of caverns cut six 'storeys' deep into the ground. It was air-conditioned, with shower-baths and cinemas. Troops moved by electric trains to giant concrete forts on the surface. Food and water stores ensured the French army could go without supplies for at least three months. There would be, wrote a journalist, 'no more bloody, muddy trenches' as in 1914–18. The Line was not extended north-westwards because of the cost, and because it would offend the Belgians. The Maginot Line gave the French a comfortable sense of security. Pleas from a certain Colonel de Gaulle that tanks be formed into units capable of moving swiftly onto the offensive were dismissed. Yet it is arguable that a lightning tank thrust into the Rhineland in 1936 might have changed the history of the world.

2 Social malaise

The *bourgeoisie*, with all its wealth and talent, had in the century up to 1914 regarded itself as the successors to the ancient ruling aristocracy of France. But after the war of 1914–18 the *bourgeoisie* felt very much less confident. Inflation, and especially the refusal of the Soviet Russian governments after 1917 to pay interest on the huge loans made by Frenchmen to the Czar, struck hard at their wealth. People began

The Maginot Line: shown here is part of the vast underground communications between the surface forts

hoarding gold and even bank notes (26,000 million francs-worth of notes 'disappeared' from circulation between 1928 and 1932). Merchants and bankers seemed unwilling to take the usual business risks. France's population was still not increasing, so it was argued that there was little point in showing confidence in the future. The Blum government of 1936 was the last straw – it represented all that the well-to-do in France despaired of. Paul Reynaud, a leading politician, remarked, 'The *bourgeoisie* seems to be contemplating its own funeral.'

3 Political instability

The effort to produce a stable pattern of governments defeated nearly all politicians in the '20s and '30s. Only Poincaré and Auguste Briand had had any success in the late 'twenties; they died in the early 'thirties, old men realising that most of what they had done for France was in a shambles. Clemenceau, who died in 1929 aged eighty-eight, was even more embittered. In his retirement he said, 'Everything I have done has been wasted. In twenty years France will be dead.' As the old guard of politicians passed away, new, untried figures emerged, but few had the leadership and statesmanlike qualities needed. Many were old, some vain, most were mediocre. None could find a policy acceptable to the French Assembly for more than a short time. The historian, Alistair Horne, who has written about the decline of France in these years, says: 'Like amoebae, parties divided and re-divided within themselves. For many politicians self-interest came to be their guiding star. A mad game of musical chairs ensued, to be played at a giddier rate until Hitler's Panzer tanks finally stopped the music in 1940.' The man who led France in the closing years of the 1930s, Edouard Daladier, was an expert in political musical chairs, but little else. He tried to be firm, but always withdrew if the pressure increased. His supporters nicknamed him 'the Bull', but a British general who knew him well acidly remarked, 'His horns bore more resemblance to the soft feelers of the snail than to the harder, bovine variety.'

4 Economic decline

Over-riding all these reasons was the long-term inability of France to grow rich and pay her way in the world. It could be argued that with the rising prosperity of the late 'twenties, France's moneyed classes, politicians and generals should have had more confidence in the future, and money to spend on defence and to invest in social and economic reforms. The confidence, however, did not survive the Depression. France now seemed a nation of old men and widows, and the arguments of the late nineteenth century were revived – with a static population who would buy any extra produce? Agriculture especially suffered. It had been slow to modernise its methods, so much so that in key crop yields like cereals and potatoes, it was the least efficient in western Europe. (The Dutch, for instance, could produce twice as much wheat as a French farm on the same sized plot.) The Paris Basin had some large, efficient farms, but the mass of peasantry toiled excessively on their small plots.

Apart from the new industries which had prospered in the late 'twenties, French manufacturing was still organised on a small scale. Two and a half million workers were employed in little craft workshops with no more than ten employees. Machinery was getting old as few employers were willing to pay for new equipment. This 'under-industrialisation' as it is called, had terrible consequences when the French tried to rearm rapidly in the face of Hitler's threats.

Lack of investment appeared to be the key to France's problems, and here the real cause of difficulty was that the French franc was over-valued. This meant that in relation to other currencies, the pound sterling or the dollar, French prices were too high, and a French manufacturer wishing to export his goods found foreign firms able to charge less for their goods; at the same time foreign goods imported into France were cheaper. Yet French politicians and businessmen were unwilling to do anything about it – they thought tampering with money values would bring unrest and possibly revolution, which would open the gates for a communist take-over.

It is easy for historians now to describe the state France was in by the end of the 1930s because they are able to take into account all the evidence which has come to light since then. In the 1930s, though, only a few Frenchmen suspected how economically stunted France had become between the wars.

The Second World War began on 1 September 1939 when German forces invaded Poland. Hitler seemed in no hurry to follow this up; the winter of 1939–40 proved uneventful. The French deluded themselves into thinking that perhaps a real war was not going to happen in the west. A tragic piece of wishful thinking it might have been, but it helps to explain why the swift military defeat of France in 1940 and the rapid downfall of the Third Republic were so startling and unexpected to Frenchmen at the time.

11
'The Stain of 1940'

At thirty minutes past midnight on 17 June 1940 the French government of the Third Republic asked the German invading armies for an armistice. It had taken a mere six weeks in the gloriously warm, sunny weather of spring 1940 for the Germans to inflict a staggering defeat on the French army. By the middle of July, not only had the whole of northern and western France been occupied by Germans, but the Third Republic had collapsed. A right-wing regime had been set up at Vichy to rule the remaining part of France and to help the Germans develop Hitler's New Order throughout Europe. A small group of Frenchmen, appalled at these events, resisted Vichy and the Germans either from within France or by escaping to England. This chapter and the next tells the story of the years 1940 to 1944, and suggests some of the important reasons for the military defeat and political collapse. It led Marc Bloch, one of France's most distinguished authors, who was later tortured and executed by the Nazis, to write: 'It will be many years before the stain of 1940 can be rubbed out.'

Military Débâcle

The plan of the French army to resist a German attack was based on three simple ideas. In the east, along the Franco-German frontier the strong Maginot Line and the difficult hilly country would hold back the invaders. In the north-east, along the Belgian frontier to the sea, the rest of the French army, with a little British support (the BEF), would enter Belgium, pivoting on a point near Sedan until they reached the excellent defensive line running south from Antwerp to the River Meuse. In the centre, between the end of the Maginot Line and Sedan was a gap: a small force of five divisions could hold the enemy as the heavily wooded region of the Ardennes made speed and manoeuvring virtually impossible.

The Germans, however, relied on the unexpected. On 10 May they attacked with a massive concentration of their Panzer tanks and motorised forces moving towards the River Meuse at Sedan, and just to the north. It was a bold move depending on efficiency and speed, and showing little respect for the accepted theory that tanks could not move

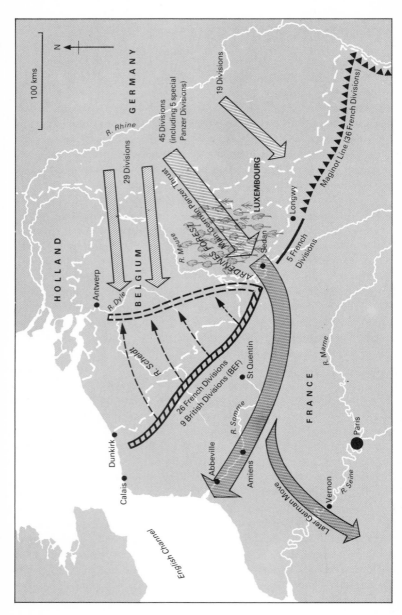

The German invasion of France in 1940

through the Ardennes. This plan was carried out by a group of able commanders of which one was the plan's author, General Heinz Guderian. He had convinced Hitler, against the advice of some senior officers, that with a sudden blow he would shatter the French line. He would then move westwards in a 250-kilometre dash for the coast, thus splitting the enemy in two and hemming one section against the Channel coast. The prize was great, but the plan had obvious risks: a concentrated French counter-attack with tanks might cut the Panzers off from their slower moving infantry support behind.

What happened can be seen by following the fortunes of one small part of the German invasion – Guderian's XIX Panzer Corps. In two days it was through the Ardennes forest and onto the banks of the Meuse at Sedan. On 13 May, with Stuka dive-bomber support, it crossed the river, but only with some foot-soldiers in rubber dinghies. The night of 13–14 May was crucial. The Germans were feverishly building pontoon bridges to get their tanks across, and victory depended on those bridges. At 11 pm the French HQ received confusing reports on exactly where the Germans were; at 1.30 am the French ordered a counter-attack – 'for dawn at 4 am'. The margin of time was now of the utmost importance. Dawn came, yet the French were not ready. At 6 am the German engineers finished and the first of Guderian's tanks rolled across. At 7 am the French attacked, and ran straight into the Panzers, for which they were unprepared. The French infantry made a hasty retreat with scenes of wild disorder in a few places. Their commander was dismayed. 'Left to themselves', he said, 'the troops dissolved, frightened by a menace that did not exist.' Guderian's tanks now began a race for the sea. By 18 May they were halfway, at St Quentin; two days later they were in Amiens and Abbeville. In eleven days the Germans had moved 350 kilometres.

If the confidence of the French High Command was under strain, Hitler's was none too good. 'The Führer is frightfully nervous', wrote one of his generals on 17 May. Hitler's concern was the left flank of Guderian's advancing Panzers. Not all the French army would behave like the troops at Sedan. One man, Colonel de Gaulle, had hastily assembled a few hundred tanks and struck northwards towards St Quentin. But he was given no air or infantry support by his senior commanders. 'We were like lost children thirty kilometres in front,' de Gaulle said. The French effort consisted merely of isolated and piecemeal attacks.

There was now a pause. The Germans regrouped and argued about how to deal with the British and French forces who were trapped between them and the sea. They argued too long. A third of a million escaped by sea from Dunkirk to England in one of the most incredible small-boat operations in history. But the French army made no use of the respite. Its commander, General Gamelin, was dismissed by Paul Reynaud, the French premier. His successor, General Weygand, made two fatal decisions. Having been told that 'all is a matter of hours', he delayed several days whilst he toured the front. Then, when he did act, he stretched out his forces into a thinly held line along the Somme. De Gaulle pleaded with Weygand to concentrate France's remaining 1,200 tanks with infantry support just to the north of Paris. 'At least', he said

French refugess escaping westwards in June 1940. All a family's moveable possessions would be in the pram

later, 'we would have had a battle, instead of a débâcle.' His plea was ignored. On 5 June the Germans resumed their offensive southwards. Within a week they were through and had crossed the Seine at Vernon. Paris fell on the 14 June. There was no 'miracle of the Marne' as in 1914. The capital city had only 700,000 people left out of 5 million. The rest had joined the horde of 8 million refugees (2 million were Belgian) strung out on the roads to the south and west. Belongings were packed on the roofs of cars, in prams and wheelbarrows. The authorities had not expected such a pitiful flight. Food, drink and lodging soon ran out; the roads became choked, and car speeds were 40 kilometres *a day*. The army itself was now in retreat; efforts by some officers to halt their men and fight were resisted by local civilians. At Poitiers, whilst soldiers were digging defences, the mayor drove out with a white flag to surrender the town to the Germans.

Political Crisis

Paul Reynaud's government was in confusion. It left Paris on 10 June for the Loire valley as part of a planned move to Bordeaux. But Reynaud's ministers, intending to meet at Tours, found great difficulty in travelling along roads clogged with refugees. Eventually they were lodged in the scattered chateaux of the Loire, but found themselves as much out of touch with the rapidly changing conditions as the refugees. One observer wrote: 'There was only one antiquated telephone in each castle (usually in the downstairs toilet), connected only with the nearest village, where the operator insisted on taking off the customary two hours for lunch and closing down at 6 pm.' General Spears, the British liaison officer, was alarmed. At his chateau the influence of Countess Hélene de Portes, Reynaud's mistress, was much in evidence: 'In the courtyard I saw to my utter astonishment, Madame de Portes in a dressing gown over red pyjamas directing the traffic. A madhouse!', Spears said.

A hastily arranged war council and a stormy cabinet meeting took place at Tours on the 13 June. Churchill flew in from Britain to find Reynaud 'depressed' and other French leaders talking of 'the hopelessness of resistance'. The influence of Hélene de Portes was almost sinister: 'Tell Paul we must give up', she told a French journalist. Reynaud pleaded for more British help, especially aircraft. The military leaders continued to disagree. De Gaulle wanted clear orders given for a retreat to Brittany where a stand would be made. But Weygand had no time for 'this arrogant man'. Weygand wanted to surrender, and his view was echoed by the eighty-four-year old, much-respected hero of Verdun, Pétain. 'Armistice is the necessary condition for the perpetuity of eternal France,' he said.

The next day political and military leaders set out for Bordeaux. As they straggled into the city, the atmosphere of despair grew worse. Albert Lebrun, President of the Republic, now agreed with Weygand and Pétain. Speaking of the 'uselessness' of the struggle, he said 'an end must be made'. Reynaud made one last effort, suggesting a retreat to France's North African colonies. He failed. Half of his ministers, his senior generals, and his mistress all wanted an armistice. He resigned at 8 pm on 16 June. Pétain took over and four and a half hours later asked the Germans for an armistice.

Explanations

Two threads, both needing explanation, run through the story of May and June 1940: the battlefield defeat of the French army, and the quite separate issue of the political pessimism which produced the armistice.

Frenchmen argued passionately about the 1940 débâcle for several years; they sought scapegoats and there was plenty of mud-slinging. Some blamed the birthrate: how could a nation of 40 million take on another of 70 million? Many examined economic performance: Germany, they argued, had overwhelming superiority in equipment because she produced, for instance, twice as much steel, and ten times as much chemicals for explosives as France. Foreigners came in for some blame: they could not be relied on. The last war's ally, America, offered only useless sympathy; and as for Britain, its BEF was too small, its RAF too concerned with home defence. Pétain said this was only to be expected – had not Napoleon I been right when he called her *'perfide albion'*, unfaithful Britain? Pétain summarised all these points later in 1940 when he broadcast to the French people: 'Too few children, too few arms, too few allies, these are the causes of our defeat.' There were grains of truth in what he said, but it was also convenient propaganda – no one was named, so he could make a more effective plea for national unity. Historians since have sifted masses of evidence and suggested explanations which in 1940 had been only partly clear, were deliberately concealed or were ignored.

First, on the battlefield the Germans did not have a real superiority until *after* Dunkirk. The battle for France was won by military skill, especially in the use of tanks. The French had 3,000 tanks to the German 2,700; but the French used theirs like horses, as mechanical chargers working closely with foot soldiers along a continuous defensive line. The Germans had other ideas, which they found in the writings of three men, Captain Liddell Hart and Major-General Fuller of Britain and, ironically, a Frenchman, Colonel Charles de Gaulle! Ignored by the French High Command, their ideas were put into practice by Heinz Guderian on the Meuse at Sedan. He concentrated his tanks into special armoured divisions (Panzers) which could punch a hole through the enemy line; then with great speed they moved to the enemy's rear, not to kill, but to confuse and terrify, until rumour produced panic.

Secondly, at no time was the contest really hopeless, despite the despairing remarks of leading French politicians and army officers. Weygand had only been Commander-in-Chief for six days before complaining, 'I am helpless; I have no reserves'. But the reality of the situation was nothing like so pessimistic. In parts of France General Spears found 'that all the horrible defeatism in high places was being redeemed by the simple heroism of the common soldier and regimental officer'. Weygand's argument that he had no reserves was nonsense: in the Maginot Line there were many men awaiting proper leadership. And France still had aircraft – Spears noticed 200 of them at Tours, but they had been given no specific duties.

Thirdly, there was nothing inevitable about the armistice. Reynaud had suggested Brittany and North Africa as sites for regrouping and organising a comeback. He was ignored because certain leading men believed they could further their political aims by signing an armistice with Germany. De Gaulle said later that the fall of France came from a far-reaching conspiracy by the enemies of the Third Republic, but, on the evidence, this idea of an elaborate plan seems far-fetched. What happened was that some men of the Right saw the defeat of the army as a magnificent opportunity to destroy the Republic and gain power. Getting rid of Reynaud and signing the armistice, were steps in that direction. Pétain made the point: 'We must wait for a French revival by remaining on the spot, rather than reconquering our territory with allied guns.' Reynaud must, of course, share some of the blame for what happened in 1940. He failed to give France the inspired, committed leadership it needed.

At the time many Frenchmen supported Pétain. They were bewildered by the sheer speed of events, and the realities were only half-glimpsed. They expected Britain to be defeated within mere months, then peace would be made. Few men, and certainly not Pétain, could have foreseen what terrors a bargain with the Nazis would bring, or that the war was far from over.

12
Vichy and the Resistance

The Fall of the Third Republic

In a clearing in a forest at Compiègne, some eighty kilometres north of Paris, Hitler led the way to a railway coach. Here on 22 June 1940 the armistice terms were to be signed. The French did not think much of Hitler's sense of history; for it was the same place and coach in which the French had received the defeated Germans in 1918. France was to be divided into two parts – the German army occupying the north and Atlantic coastal area, with Alsace-Lorraine once more a part of Germany; the French government under Pétain could keep control of the Mediterranean coast and its interior, and maintain a small army and the fleet. But 2 million French prisoners-of-war were to remain in German hands, until Britain had been defeated.

Marshal Pétain and Pierre Laval, seen here inspecting a guard of honour in Vichy

The fleet was a valuable asset to the defeated French, for it gave them at least a 'voice' in western Mediterranean affairs. Great Britain, now France's ex-ally, thought this fleet might easily fall into German hands. So the British navy in the Mediterranean moved to the Algerian coast, and after a short and confusing exchange of words with the French Pétainist authorities there, the British ships opened fire. Some important French ships were sunk in Mers-el-Kebir harbour. Anglo-French relations, already sour in the last weeks before the armistice, now became very acid indeed: the memory of this incident rankled for years.

Meanwhile the grave of the Third Republic was being dug. The French republican deputies had moved from Bordeaux to set up their government offices at Vichy, a holiday resort in the unoccupied zone. Here on 10 July they were presented with a bill by Pierre Laval, a leading supporter of Pétain: 'The National Assembly gives all powers to the authority of Marshal Pétain, A new constitution of the French State shall safeguard the rights of work, the family and the country.' It became law by 569 votes to 80. With this power Pétain and his chosen ministers were to rule France and maintain relations with Germany until August 1944.

Vichy: in Theory and Practice

Frenchmen today still regard Vichy with strong emotions. One difficulty in its controversial reputation is that what the Vichy regime became after a couple of years was not what it set out to be. Another is that the historical record became distorted after the liberation of France in 1944, when those who had resisted Vichy/German rule wrote attacks on everything Vichy had stood for. Laval, perhaps, suffered more than most. Churchill regarded him as little more than a German agent; the French politician, Vincent Auriol, wrote, 'that crook and twister. Everything about him is black – his clothes, his face, his soul.'

The truth is not so clear-cut. In putting the case for Vichy, Pétain said, 'It is the French people who, by its representatives gathered in the National Assembly on 10 July 1940, entrusted me with power.' Richard Griffiths, the biographer of Pétain, has stressed that, 'In the country as a whole enthusiasm for him was immense and the regime rested on his personality.' He represented for many Frenchmen the best of the Right, a man who would save France from the parliamentary ditherings of the Third Republic. Army officers and leading Catholics rallied around the Marshal as leader of what he called the National Revolution – its rallying cry, to replace the old republican *Liberté, Egalité, Fraternité*, was taken from the 10 July Law: *Travail, Famille, Patrie*. Thus men like Pétain, Laval and Weygand did not see the armistice as a disaster. As Laval put it, 'Any further resistance would mean the total occupation of France.' He further defended the 10 July Law: 'The majority demanded it, or it must be imagined that I had extraordinary powers of suggestion over the Assembly.' As for the future Pétain and Laval saw the Nazi Party of Germany as fellow right-wingers. In October 1940 Pétain met Hitler at Montoire. Here Pétain used a word which was to have terrible effects on France: collaboration. 'To maintain the unity of France within the New Order of Europe', he declared, 'I enter today upon the path of collaboration.'

The case against Pétain, Laval and Vichy is simple. Collaboration with the Germans proved to be a costly bargain. They expected a quick end to the Second World War, but as it dragged on so the 'terms' of German collaboration got worse. At the start many Frenchmen in occupied France were surprised at the speed with which things returned to normal. Within days of the armistice Germans bought souvenirs in Paris; *'Ici on parle allemand'* notices appeared in restaurants. In rural areas polite German soldiers paid for their drinks and eggs. But the Gestapo and the apparatus of Nazi terror and rule by compulsion had not yet arrived.

Vichy rule in the unoccupied zone soon became distasteful to many. The government disbanded trade unions and banned political parties. All officials had to take an oath of loyalty to Pétain. Vichy was also anti-semitic. All Jews were excluded from teaching and public service, and were soon to be driven from their businesses. In education the control of the Catholic Church was revived; Greek, Latin and religion occupied the main part of the curriculum. Anyone opposing these policies soon attracted the attention of the *milice*, the French Gestapo. Prefects, too, were allowed to arrest people. By 1942, 80,000 political opponents were in prison in appalling conditions. Vichy had quickly become the mirror-image of the other fascist police states of the period, Italy, Spain and Germany.

Things were much worse in the occupied zone. The French were expected to pay the costs of the German occupation, and the sums demanded mounted each year. They had to supply the German soldiers with food. The Germans formed French soldiers into units and sent them to fight alongside German army divisions in the Russian war which began in 1941. In 1942 there was a sudden increase in German control and demands: *all* France was to be occupied, and large numbers of Frenchmen were sent to work in German factories. At first Laval cooperated, and a quarter of a million Frenchmen were transported. He then tried to apply a brake; and was partly successful in that he kept women from being drafted and exempted some occupations like railway workers and miners. Yet within a year 1,300,000 Frenchmen – Laval's Labour Service, prisoners-of-war, and many from Alsace-Lorraine – had been put to work in munition factories or on farms in Germany. It was a colossal number. All over France the standard of living was sharply reduced. Food was in short supply, the rationing system allowing only 1,200 calories a day, which was under half a normal adult's needs. The Nazis frightened people into obeying them. In all, 30,000 French hostages were tortured to death or shot during the occupation years.

On balance, Vichy began in 1940 with high hopes. It blamed the inefficiencies of the old Third Republic for the defeat. There was nothing basically evil about Pétain's new government, whatever its later critics said. It was a Right-wing alternative to the mainly Left-wing republican governments which had ruled France since the 1870s. Yet Vichy stands condemned. It failed to protect its own people from the barbarities of Nazi rule. It failed to maintain for them even a moderate standard of living. Worst of all it failed in its promise of security: for each Frenchman killed in the fighting in 1940, another died as a civilian victim of the Vichy-German régime.

La Flamme de la Résistance Française

Resistance to Vichy and German occupation grew from tiny seeds. Although the enthusiasm felt in 1940 for Pétain rapidly melted, questions remained. Was Vichy *the* lawful government of France? Was it right to collaborate? Where did treason begin? Emmanuel d'Astier, later an important Resistance leader, wrote of the difficulties of getting support at the start: 'Everyone was reluctant or afraid.'

The official 'voice' of the Resistance was first heard at 6 pm on 18 June 1940 from London. General de Gaulle, having escaped to England, invited all French officers who could to join him. He spoke of 'The flame of the French Resistance; is all hope gone? Is the defeat final? No!' In view of what happened later it was an historic broadcast, but at the time he seemed a relatively unknown, rather lonely figure trying to keep his countrymen at war. The BBC did not even record the speech, and very few Frenchmen heard it; even fewer joined the defiant general.

However, as the full meaning of occupation became clear to Frenchmen, a powerful Resistance Movement grew up. Small things like directing Germans on the Paris *Métro* to stations out of their way grew into acts of sabotage. Trains were derailed; 'shock' units of thirty men became the nucleus of a secret army. These underground groups produced newspapers: one of them, *Combat*, had a circulation of 30,000 and appeared three times a month. Active Resistance leaders lived constantly in fear of torture and death, and lived away from their families, in hiding with forged papers. After 1943 support for the Resistance increased rapidly as Laval's Labour Service began to take effect and people were rounded up in the street. Many decided to 'lose themselves' in the countryside. About 100,000 eventually took to the hills and became the *maquis*, young, embittered men on whom the Resistance leaders could depend – if they could get enough arms. The RAF parachuted some, but there was rarely enough.

Gradually de Gaulle pressed all these different levels of resistance into some kind of unity. He faced great difficulties. He worked from London, where he distrusted the British, and they were not very cooperative. His first success was in getting the French African colonies to recognise him

A train after sabotage by French Resistance in the Second World War. The inset shows how saboteurs worked by fastening pieces of metal at an angle to the rail

as the real French authority, not Pétain. Then some Resistance groups accepted his leadership; *Combat* was one of the first. But communists who dominated many southern Resistance units were very suspicious of him. He was of the centre-Right; they were on the extreme Left. Although reluctantly they saw his value as someone who would bring all the groups together they remained anti-Gaullist at heart. All the groups eventually, if uneasily, united into the FFI, the French Forces of the Interior, which coordinated Resistance efforts.

For four years France had, in effect, been engaged in a savage civil war: the German-supported Vichy forces of the extreme Right versus the multi-headed Resistance forces of the Centre and Left. In 1944 Vichy had to deal with American and British Commonwealth military power as well. Already discredited, it had no chance of survival when the Germans were driven from France.

13
Liberation . . . and 'Collabos' and 'Trafiquants'

1944: France Liberated – by Whom?

The largest naval, military and air operation in history took place on
6 June 1944. This was D-Day, and the Allies' aim, with their invasion of
Normandy, was the liberation of France from German and Vichy rule.
Two million men from a dozen nations were to drive the Germans out.
American and British generals were in command of this force. Some of
them were unsure of the value of the Free French army units who had
joined the invasion force, or of the part the Resistance might play. The
Americans thought an allied military committee would be the only
possible government to replace Vichy; they were very suspicious of de
Gaulle, 'that prickly general', and the Resistance leaders were mostly
unknown to them.

Yet the part played by the Resistance was valuable – General
Eisenhower, the Allied Supreme Commander, later estimated that the
200,000 fighters who rose up all over France in the summer of 1944 were
worth fifteen army divisions and shortened the war by two months.
Their disruption of communications was a key factor. One particular
operation so hampered the movement of a powerful German SS
Division that it took nine days instead of three to get from Toulouse in
the south to Normandy. Though of great value to the Allies, the cost in
human terms was appalling – at Oradour, near Limoges, its 600
inhabitants were burned alive in the village church by the SS as reprisal
for the delay.

Whilst the main allied effort was in the north, the Resistance
managed to take over complete control in the south-west. Here
communists were strong, and they took immediate revenge on the
Vichy officials in a short reign of terror. This did not happen in the
north. De Gaulle had laid his plans well. A week after D-Day he visited
the army bridgeheads in Normandy, and left behind his chosen officials
who followed on the heels of the allied armies taking over the local
administration of the sub-prefectures.

De Gaulle not only had to persuade the British and Americans that *he*
represented France; he knew the communist liberation committees in
the south would challenge his authority now that the Resistance work

was over, and he had many rivals elsewhere in France. But Paris was the bedrock of authority; he had to be accepted there. As the allies approached the city, liberation committees there began to fight the Germans on their own. The fighting was confused, with little cooperation between the communist and non-communist members of the Resistance. At least 1,500 died. But the French were lucky. The German military commander, General von Choltitz, disobeyed Hitler's personal order to raze Paris to the ground. In the confusion de Gaulle persuaded the allies that a purely French armoured division should take the city. General Leclerc's tanks then led a Gaullist-controlled entry, and Choltitz surrendered.

The next day, the 25 August 1944, de Gaulle arrived to supervise the new government of Paris at the Hôtel de Ville. People have rightly judged this as one of the great moments of recent French history. The enthusiasm was enormous. An American wrote later, 'We were marching twenty-four abreast down the Champs Elysées; the whole street was jammed with people, laughing and yelling and crying and singing. They were throwing flowers at us and bringing us bottles of wine.'

'Collabos' and Traitors

Some Frenchmen had suffered greatly because of the collaboration of others with the Germans. It was inevitable that there would be a settling of accounts. Some of it was rough justice. In the south hundreds of prominent *collabos* had already been executed without a proper trial. All over France women who had been 'too friendly' with Germans were seized and their heads were shaven. The economic *collabos*, who had traded with the Germans, were more difficult to get at. A newspaper expressed the resentment: 'They have made millions. They bought themselves chateaux, furs and gold. In the hungry and blacked out Paris of the Occupation they feasted behind the curtains of the night clubs.'

Of the official trials, which included members of the *milice*, the two most sensational concerned Pétain and Laval. There was plenty of personal hatred as leading figures of the Third Republic gave evidence. A Resistance hero pointed an accusing finger at Pétain, and said, 'If there remains in him even a little love for France, let him, before he pays with his life, fall to his knees and ask her pardon.' Was Pétain guilty of treason? Léon Blum was in no doubt. 'Treason,' he declared, 'is the act of selling out' – and Pétain had done just this. Volumes of evidence were produced for his eighteen-day trial, including a letter to Hitler. One sentence seemed to seal Pétain's fate: 'France,' he told the Führer, 'preserves the memory of your noble gesture' (i.e. for allowing Vichy to be established). It was obvious too that he regarded a German victory as inevitable. This proof of his part in the events of 1940 shocked many people. Pétain made a desperate plea: 'With a knife at my throat, I struggled against enemy demands.' But he was sentenced to death; in view of his great age, it was changed to life imprisonment.

If Pétain was given some respect, Laval received none. He became the scapegoat for all the evils of the Vichy years. In a noisy trial, Laval was insulted and screamed at by the jury – one juror promising him 'twelve shots in the skin'. Laval, sentenced to death, tried to poison himself; but he was revived, then taken out of his cell and shot.

The purge of *collabos* and traitors slowly petered out. Only 767 were shot after official trials, but the number who were executed privately

Young women who became too friendly with German soldiers were persecuted as collaborators. The Resistance shaved the hair of this French girl whose baby's father was a German

and in cold blood will probably never be known. A British historian, Alfred Cobban, says the evidence points to about 30,000.

The Fourth Republic

The Third Republic had 'died' in 1940. For four years loyalties in France had been deeply divided, and the long-standing rivalries of Left and Right worsened. It was very much due to General de Gaulle that Liberation was not followed by civil war and chaos. Now, whilst his personal reputation stood high in the minds and hearts of many Frenchmen, he faced two tasks: international recognition and the framing of a government. With the war stretching on into 1945 he had difficulty in getting Britain, the USA and Russia to treat France as a great power. The allies were slow to equip the revived French army, and de Gaulle was rarely invited to the crucial conferences that were

General de Gaulle touring France after the Liberation seen here visiting a small town

deciding the fate of the world after the war. At home, there was the powerful Communist Party, whose leader, Maurice Thorez, had spent the war years in Moscow. De Gaulle had no intention of letting France break up into a patchwork of local 'soviet republics'; he wanted to revive the old system of powerful centralised rule from Paris.

In 1945 a general election was held. There was no question of bringing the old Third Republic back, so the new Assembly would have the task of working out a constitution. The communists were very strong, having a quarter of the votes, but for the first time in French history women voted, and many gave their support to a new political party, the MRP, led by a group of progressive Catholics. Finding himself at the head of a parliamentary government was not to de Gaulle's liking. He wanted to be a strong president[1] who could decide policy, rather like American presidents, yet he discovered he could not take a step without the consent of the many big party groups in the Assembly. Relations became strained. In the midst of arguments about a new constitution, de Gaulle, by now quite exasperated with having his ideas questioned, suddenly, on 20 January 1946, resigned and announced he would retire from politics to write his memoirs. This was a spectacular moment in French politics. Some of de Gaulle's colleagues forecast a perilous future after the departure of the 'male Joan of Arc'.

Even with de Gaulle gone, the new constitution had a difficult birth. The first draft was rejected by the French people in a referendum. A final version was accepted in October 1946 by the narrowest of margins: 9 million for, 8 million against, and $8\frac{1}{2}$ million stayed at home! Real power rested with the National Assembly, yet elections had proved that no clear-cut party majority was possible, so the prospect of rapidly changing coalitions loomed ahead. The Fourth Republic seemed to resemble the old Third all too closely.

'Trafiquants'

The legacy of the war and occupation years in France was grim. The physical destruction alone created difficulties. Rail and road transport were nearly paralysed: 1,000 bridges had been destroyed, including all those over the Seine between Paris and the sea; only 3,000 railway engines were usable out of a pre-war total of 17,000. This led to a quite ridiculous food problem. Parts of rural France had plenty to eat, yet Paris was on starvation rations. A reporter who drove out to Normandy

[1]See the guide on page 14

wrote, 'In every Norman village huge pyramids of *camembert* cheeses were getting higher and higher – in both senses – in the absence of transport.' Another result of the occupation years was the number of franc notes in circulation. 1944 had six times 1939's figure. This, with the transport problem and inefficient government rationing, created the *trafiquants*, people who made fat profits by selling food and other goods on the 'black market'.

The cities suffered most. There were rackets in everything – in meat, in newsprint, in sugar; even the police sold motor-vehicle licences 'under the counter'. There were food riots and coal riots. Near Lille in January 1945, 1,200 people invaded a coal mine and carried away 150 tons of coal. Eggs in Paris went up from five francs each to seventeen francs within two days. On average each Parisian had lost twenty kilogrammes in weight during the occupation, and was hoping for something better after the Liberation. In a hard winter, even if he could get food, there was little fuel with which to cook it. A ration of one sack of coal, promised in the month of Liberation, August '44, had not arrived in the following January. Electricity was turned off from morning to evening except for one hour at noon. 'Paris', one observer wrote, 'was restless, anxious, cantankerous.' The newspapers wrote harsh words about *trafiquants* and about peasants who 'hoarded franc notes in their washing coppers'. They always seemed to have a surplus of goods which they sold at high prices. At Christmas 1945 shops could be seen stocked high with goods for the newly-rich – the *trafiquants*. 'Nightgowns at nightmare prices', an American journalist said after looking in a Paris store.

Many people were disappointed by the failure of the government to solve the shortages and inflation. The 2 million French prisoners-of-war and deported workers, who returned home late in 1945, were shocked. One ex-prisoner wrote, 'There's a black market on every level. Only fools work.' It was to be some time before the *trafiquants* ceased to find any profit in their activities in post-war France.

1947: a Turning Point

For two years the coalition governments of the Fourth Republic had found the Communists very difficult partners. Matters came to a head in 1947. French efforts to recover her colony in Indo-China had been vigorously opposed by the Communists, and they were hostile to an American offer to help solve France's economic problems. Eventually, they were dismissed from the government. American aid, called the

Marshall Plan, was accepted and used for a recovery programme that had already been thought out. Amidst the despair of the food shortages, the onset of the Cold War, and the running sore of an Indo-China conflict, some important developments had been touched off that were to put France well on the road to recovery. Certain key industries had been given government help. A social insurance scheme promised a new security to family life. One Frenchman, Jean Monnet, had proposed a plan for long-term recovery that was to go on working quietly whilst the politicians argued. And another Frenchman, Christian Dior, restored a cherished reputation: at 10.30 am on Wednesday 12 February 1947 the Dior 'New Look' took the fashion world by storm.

Part Three
Dynamic revival 1947–76

14
New Confidence and Surging Enterprise 1947–67

Jean Monnet and the Plan

The defeat of 1940 and the war years gave some Frenchmen, inside France and in exile in Britain and the USA, an opportunity to re-think the future. They were dismayed at France's previous stalemate society, which seemed to have existed for at least half a century. They argued that there had been too much caution, even pessimism.

The years immediately after the war changed all this. The shock of 1940, Marshall Aid, a rise in the birthrate, a reappearance of French technical flair – all these helped to produce what was called 'the French economic miracle'. But one thing, perhaps even one man, provided government help to make this miracle possible. In 1946–47 Jean Monnet launched the Plan. Monnet, an outstanding economist and diplomat, was appointed by the government to be Commissioner General of a small organisation that would plan the reconstruction of the French economy. With the slogan of 'modernisation or downfall', his ideas quietly but efficiently penetrated French industry and business. He gave control of key industries to technocrats – men who combined the talents and training of an engineer, civil servant and businessman. Monnet himself worked through a secretariat of about forty young, clever men from the universities, civil service and industry. They set targets for growth in all parts of the French economy. Then they met at a round-table conference with all the heads of firms and trade union leaders to thrash out how to achieve the target in, say, pig-breeding or aluminium production. To encourage firms to work with the Plan, Monnet had a series of rewards which included tax reliefs, extra loans and valuable government contracts. The Plan faced huge difficulties. The politicians of the Fourth Republic still played their political games. For years vast sums of money went, not to industry, but

The appalling devastation of the War, seen here at St. Lô in Normandy. The top picture shows the destruction around the church in a 1945 aerial photograph. The same view with the church clear in the centre is shown in 1955 after an impressive reconstruction programme

to the army to pay for colonial wars in Indo-China and Algeria. And Monnet had to fight hard to get money for the most important heavy industries of steel and electricity – the politicians much preferred to put money into the more popular, vote-catching consumer goods. Also some industries and some areas of France modernised swiftly, others slowly, some not at all. A few observant commentators likened French recovery to an over-powerful engine in a rickety car.

Trains, Cars, Planes and Ships

Transport showed the merits of the Plan to the full. Monnet decided to link French flair and ingenuity to the desperate economic need for an efficient communications system.

The sheer scale of wartime destruction of railway engines and rolling stock was a blessing in disguise to Louis Armand, the technocrat who became head of the French State Railways in 1946. He refused to re-open uneconomic lines. He had new marshalling yards planned with the latest electronic devices. He insisted on modern diesel and electric engines. A programme of staff reductions, Armand's most controversial measure, was begun. Within two decades the French railway system became famous for technical progress and efficiency. Its electric engines reached world record times of 330 kph, and it developed hovercraft-like aerotrains. Its car-carrying services and glass-roofed panoramic coaches attracted the tourist trade. Another success was its small, two-coach diesel trains for rapid cross-country connections, giving a useful and inexpensive service to rural areas. Armand had no real problems with over-manning, with urban bottlenecks where road and railway builders competed with house builders to buy land, or with the expensive carriage of small loads over short distances – problems which plagued some of France's neighbours, particularly Britain. French worries were almost exclusively financial. A big deficit built up in the late 1960s, due to the heavy cost of modern equipment and to the lump-sums paid out to redundant rail workers – those who were put out of work as Armand's plan took shape.

Another success story concerned cars. The French automobile industry had enjoyed a high reputation since the beginning of the century. One firm, Renault, had forty years experience behind it. But in 1944, Louis Renault was charged with collaboration with the Nazis, and had his 'empire' confiscated by the state. An idealistic technocrat, Pierre Dreyfus, soon became its manager. He believed every family had a 'right' to own a car, and to this end he encouraged the production of a remarkably cheap baby car, the 4CV (*quatre chevaux* or four horse power). As French prosperity grew the 4CV gave way in 1956 to one of the most successful cars ever made, the Dauphine, which sold over 2 million models. The Renault works at Billancourt, near Paris, enjoyed an almost strike-free labour-relations record: regular wage increases, housing and social clubs were promised in return for uninterrupted work. Citroën, an independent car company, also had its top selling models. They were built to last, and its 2CV, beginning life in 1948, was still producing over 200,000 twenty years later. One observer commented: 'It looks like an old tin can, rarely breaks down, costs hardly anything, and does eighty kilometres to the gallon.' France built a reputation on models like these, and on other tough and elegant ones. Not only does France have today the highest number of car-owners in Europe, but by 1966 she had overtaken Britain in production and exports.

Equally brilliant was the French recovery of their impressive pre-war record in aviation. One company and one man led the way. In 1946 Georges Héreil was put in charge of Sud-Est Aviation at Toulouse. His job was not an easy one, as the USA controlled ninety per cent of the world air transport market. Héreil planned a fast, medium-range jet airliner in 1952. Careful testing at all stages would be required, because the British *Comet* which had seemed to lead the world in the early 'fifties suffered two sensational crashes, as a result of metal fatigue. Héreil decided not to rush his programme. When in 1959 his superb *Caravelle* went into service, it was an immediate success. It was silent, comfortable, and could travel at 800 kph. 270 *Caravelles* were sold to thirty-four of the world's airlines in ten years. By then,

An Air France 'Caravelle' airliner taking off from Orly Airport in Paris in 1961

Sud-Est had become Aérospatiale, and in partnership with the British Aircraft Corporation, had produced another technological triumph, the Anglo-French *Concorde*.

Some of the French transport ideas of the 1950s were being used merely to boost prestige in the 'sixties. *Concorde* research costs soon reached £500 million, five times the original estimates, and many people called for it to be cancelled in 1964–65. (It continued a status-symbol which, when it was launched commercially in 1976, was unlikely ever to recover the £1,000 million invested in it.) A passenger-liner, the 55,000 tonne *France*, launched at St Nazaire in 1962, was also accused of being built for prestige. For some years it made good profits shipping American tourists across the Atlantic, but many Frenchmen argue that its huge investment of state money could have been better spent on housing and other social needs.

Fuel and Power

In the twentieth century energy resources (fuel and power) have become the key to a country's international prestige and independence. For France with her rapid growth of industry and prosperity it was vital that adequate supplies be available, cheaply and under her control. She worked hard towards this dream, but it proved only partially possible to fulfil.

The government gave priority to coal production, and output increased at an encouraging rate; however French coal is inferior in quality to that of Poland, the USA and Britain, and as industries began to buy more foreign coal and oil, coal-mining became uneconomical in the 1960s. It seemed more promising to develop electricity and a giant, forty-year investment programme was launched in 1946. Within half that time it had paid off spectacularly. Thirty dams were built in the Alps, Pyrenees and Massif Central to tap France's rich hydro-electric resources: the Tignes Dam on the River Isère, for instance, was an engineering triumph, helping the electricity industry keep pace with a demand which doubled every decade! France's most famous and ingenious power project was the world's first tidal dam across the River Rance between St Malo and Dinard in Brittany. Opened in 1966, it used a strong, twelve-metre high tide to extract electric power both as the tide rose and as it ebbed. The road across the top and its design attracted tourists and publicity, but it produced only 0.5 per cent of French electricity consumption. It had none of the practical value of some of the Alpine dams, and like *Concorde*, it seemed to be a great technological achievement with doubtful economic prospects.

Much more useful was the natural gas found in the Pyrenean foothills near Pau in 1951. *Le gaz de Lacq* became a well-organised operation and within twenty years supplied France with a third of her gas consumption. The huge, 575 hectare site of multi-coloured pipes was a most brilliant fiery scene at night as security flares lit up the sky all round the Pau plain. A valuable by-product from the gas, sulphur, led the scheme to be a remarkably clean, economic industrial enterprise. Lacq grew into a matter of considerable French pride and typified the French economic resurgence.

Oil and nuclear power schemes were not so straightforward. Both were caught up in political arguments and prestige-hunting rivalries. Algerian oil gave France forty per cent of her needs, but Algeria's long and bloody struggle for independence between 1954 and 1962 meant that supplies were always dependent on political and military considerations. The French government tried to become independent of the powerful international oil companies like the American Esso and the Anglo-Dutch Shell. This led in 1966 to new ideas, such as the marketing of Elf, a French brand of petrol. In the 1960s, too, France tried to go-it-alone in nuclear power. Expensive projects gave France some prestige, but by the end of the decade only three per cent of her electricity came from this source.

Dior and the 'New Look'

French industry had traditionally laid as much importance on luxury products as on basic commodities. After the Second World War her reputation in *haute couture* needed to be revived. This, dating back to Worth in the nineteenth century, had been improved by such names as Paul Poiret in the early 1900s and Gabrielle 'Coco' Chanel in the 'thirties. Poiret, for instance, claimed that he heralded modern fashion with his famous declaration in 1908, 'In the name of Liberty, I freed the bust.' Chanel, too, startled the fashion-conscious with her 'sweater lines', pleated skirts, and her world-famous perfume, Chanel No. 5.

In February 1947 Paris recovered her reputation in a confident and dramatically successful way, when Christian Dior paraded his 'New Look' fashion. It was well timed – just when women were seeking to get away from the war-time, almost military, square-shoulder styles and the narrow, short, austerity clothing, Dior announced: 'I design clothes for flower-like women, with rounded shoulders, full, feminine busts, above enormous spreading skirts which come to

well below the calves.' Dior was a meticulous crafts-
man with considerable business talent. He was
lent money by a rich textile manufacturer,
Marcel Boussac, to open a fashion-house in 1946 with
sixty staff; the overnight success of the 'New Look'
(700 Dior suits were sold in London's West End
stores in two weeks) led to a steady expansion,
and six years later he was employing a thousand
people in twenty-eight workrooms. His fashion
empire extended world-wide to include dresses,
furs, stockings and perfume, before his death
in 1957.

Paris, of course, had other eminent names – Fath,
Balmain, Balenciaga – but after Dior's death all
the fashion houses were challenged by fierce foreign
competition. In the 1960s Mary Quant and the 'mini-skirt' destroyed
French exclusiveness. Parisian *haute couture* wilted, and by the late
'sixties French designers like Yves St Laurent were promoting ready-to-
wear clothes. French fashion was still powerful, but no longer
dominant.

Hypermarchés versus the Little Shops

For over a century French shops were of two kinds, both with the same
ideas on profits. There was the small retail shop, either specialising in
one product in the towns or selling most things in rural areas. There was
also the modern department store, which France had introduced to the
world when Bon Marché was opened in Paris in 1852. Both kinds hated
cut-throat competition. They preferred selling fewer expensive goods
with a large profit on each article, which made prices in France very high.

Into this cosy world came a young Brittany grocer, Edouard Leclerc,
who, in 1949, began offering discount prices. He bought directly from a
producer in bulk, and sold at prices which allowed only low profits. He
relied on the belief that low prices would lead to rapid sales. Traditional
shops tried to force him out of business by making illegal agreements
with manufacturers in which they agreed not to sell to Leclerc at lower
prices. So Leclerc successfully appealed to the government, who, in
1953, banned agreements to keep prices high. Leclerc's methods,
coupled with this government measure, were the basis for a shopping
revolution in the 1960s. In 1957 the first supermarket was opened;
twelve years later there were a thousand, and this number doubled in

the next three years. The really big ones were called *hypermarchés*, an idea of Marcel Fournier, whose chain, Carréfour, first began in southern Paris in 1963. Later a massive one was planned for Marseille with 22,000 square metres of selling space; it became the largest shop in Europe, selling anything from TV sets and suits to caviar and frozen snails, and staying open until 10 pm.

Enterprise and confidence had changed yet another area of traditional French industrial and commercial practice. Not all Frenchmen saw this as progress. Toulouse had six hypermarkets built around it. Few made adequate profits. It all seemed Americanisation gone mad. Also petty crime such as shop-lifting increased dramatically. Worse still was the slow death of the small shop. By the end of the 1960s over half of France's 370,000 food shops were small, family affairs only just managing to scrape a living. Little, too, had been done to modernise the distribution of food. The movement of meat and vegetables was dreadfully congested throughout the 1950s and '60s. Only in 1968 were schemes in Paris designed to ease this serious problem.

Le Bébé-Boom and Women's Rights

In seeking explanations of French recovery in the period 1947–67 French writers on population matters point to a welcome rise in the birthrate as one of the vital factors. The population rose from 40 million

Carréfour's gigantic hypermarket on the rural outskirts of Chartres in north-east France, opened in the early 1960s

in 1946 to more than 50 million in 1968. Historians have suggested two reasons for what its critics call 'a policy of national rabbitism'. First, various ideas for family allowances, paid by the government according to the number of children, were brought together in 1939 in a *Code de la Famille* and extended after the war. These child allowances were the highest in Europe, often as much as thirty per cent of a worker's income. Secondly, it was clear that the French people were regaining a faith in the future. The results of *le bébé-boom* were far-reaching. It provided a future work-force and a future market which were the necessary incentive to increase production. It also gave the French authorities new problems: young people needed schools, social services and housing, and as they grew up some became very critical of the old traditions in French life. As one writer put it, 'Baby-making became a prestige industry, and *la jeunesse* a national slogan.' Not that the young were taken in by this: they felt that authorities paid only lip-service to their needs. In 1968, as we shall see, these tensions came to a head.

Women, too, sought to gain from freer attitudes in society. They seemed to have little interest in politics. Having been given the vote in 1944, the majority voted the same way as their husbands; and in 1967 the National Assembly had only eleven women deputies. But in some fields there was a move towards equal opportunity. Unmarried daughters of the *bourgeoisie* were now expected to look for a job. The number of female students at universities rose until, in the late 1960s, they were forty-seven per cent of total numbers. The 1964 Matrimonial Act removed most of the legal inequalities between husband and wife. (Women no longer needed a husband's permission to open a bank account and obtain a passport, and in divorce proceedings they were given equal rights.) In other areas women's rights were still heavily restricted. Ideas that, even in *le bébé-boom*, a woman might want to plan her family were not encouraged by the Church and the government. A 1920 law banning birth control was challenged in 1956 by Madame Weill-Halle, who opened a family-planning clinic at Grenoble. She had to carry on a difficult campaign for eleven years before she got the 1920 law repealed.

'France marries her century'

Between 1947 and 1967 France had, as de Gaulle put it, leapt forward economically and socially 'to marry her century'. At last France was enjoying that prosperity and faith in the future which other industrialised countries had had for fifty to a hundred years.

Government statistics for September 1968 revealed that the average French worker's income had doubled in twenty years; cars, TV sets, summer holidays by the sea were no longer *bourgeois* privileges. In the period 1954 to 1968 the percentage of homes with refrigerators rose from seven to sixty-four; with television from one to fifty-three; with cars from twenty-one to forty-eight. The sea and the mountains were the setting for a great revival in sport – in those taking part even more than as spectators. Frenchmen owned 20,000 private sailing and motor yachts in 1960: nine years later the figure was 233,000! Grenoble grew into a large town, partly because it was near the Alpine skiing resorts – over a million went to the slopes every years. Olympic skiing champions, like Jean-Claude Killy in 1968, were national idols. The Tour-de-France cycle race and league football, always popular, became mammoth spectator sports.

Some Frenchmen had reservations about what 'marrying her century' had done to France. The eagerness for material goods had too much Americanisation about it, from which many recoiled in horror. Traditional French culture found in difficult to flourish in this atmosphere; there was no parallel in painting and music to compare with the *belle époque*.

Only in the cinema could Paris rightly claim to be still the cultural capital of the West. The *nouvelle vague*, or New Wave, of French film directors created a cinema-in-bloom in the 1950s and '60s. The French disliked the American ideas of popular commercial films with 'stars' released through multiple cinema circuits. They believed that a film was a personal creation. It was defined like this in a 1948 manifesto of the *nouvelle vague:* 'The film is a form through which an artist can express his thoughts or translate his obsessions, just like a novel.' Directors like Alan Resnais and Robert Bresson became household words in France with their personal, often controversial films. Another, Jean-Luc Godard, was greeted by critics as the most remarkable director in European film-making since the Second World War. One of his films, *Alphaville*, made in 1965, pin-pointed the fears which Frenchmen had about the modernisation programmes. Set in a 1984-style future, it concerned the destruction of the human soul and emotion by computers and planners; what alarmed Parisians was their recognition that much of the photography of a soulless city of machines was actually taken in parts of modern Paris. As Godard said, 'The job of artists like me is to set ambushes for planners. We can't hope to win – but we can delay things.'

15
Politicians Argue . . . Meanwhile an Empire Crumbles

A Private Game Called 'The System'

Although the late 'forties and 'fifties saw a remarkable recovery in French economic and social life, it was equally remarkable that politicians seemed hardly to have changed at all in their methods and aims. As one wit put it in 1948 'The Fourth Republic is dead; it has been succeeded by the Third.' No single political party ever attracted a big majority of voters – thus every government had to be a coalition. Parties in France were quite unlike those in Britain. There were a great many of them, they were smaller, less well organised, and much poorer. Governments were never elected on a party programme, which the voters might expect to be put into practice; the only hope of ever doing anything lay in bargaining with other small parties in the Assembly, which meant, of course, compromising on policies. A government when it was formed often put forward policies which bore little resemblance to the general election result.[1]

The average voter in provincial France was quite disillusioned. To him politicians were conducting their own private game in remote Paris. As father and grandfather had mistrusted governments in the Third Republic, so also was the son wary of them in the Fourth. 'Government' in rural France meant two things: visits from the tax-collector, or the arrival of the recruiting-sergeant! De Gaulle summed up the situation: he called the endless private game of the politicians 'The System'.

The Parties

The complications of French parties were made worse by some political groups refusing to call themselves parties at all. De Gaulle's supporters in 1945 took this attitude. Parties and coalitions, they concluded, had been an important reason for the Third Republic's weakness – now, with a powerful leader and a great cause, that of restoring *la gloire* to France, they thought all Frenchmen ought to support de Gaulle. Although he officially retired from political life in 1946, his supporters

[1]See the guide on page 14.

in the National Assembly, the Gaullists, were sure he would return. They were right – eventually. But meanwhile their support in the country dwindled, and the number of Gaullist deputies fell from over 100 in 1950 to only 21 in 1956.

The political views of the Gaullists were on the Right, though they were not extreme. A new party was formed in 1944 with powerful support from young Catholics, called the MRP or Christian Democrats. It was just Right of Centre. At times it attracted many voters, but they fell away a little in the 'fifties when the party seemed to become part of The System, which it had so bitterly attacked when it was formed. The big Centre-Left party, the Radicals, was also losing support. Having dominated the Assemblies from 1900 to 1940, its support from the mass of peasants and small businessmen fell away. As a party it proved too timid, both in a crisis and in dealing with some urgent domestic problems. It was said that the party had 'no funds, no soul and no ideas'.

On the Left, the Socialist Party in 1945 had a big following; this also steadily declined from $4\frac{1}{2}$ to $2\frac{3}{4}$ million voters within six years. It had always claimed to be a revolutionary party, and looked back to Léon Blum's Popular Front of 1936 for inspiration, yet its leadership, under Guy Mollet, grew too moderate for its supporters. Its chance of reviving French political life evaporated.

The French Communist Party, the PCF, was a distinct group with a strong party organisation and policy. It had a large following, and its reputation stood high after the part it had played in the Resistance during the war. It captured twenty-six per cent of the votes in the 1945 election, and took part in the coalition government. It was an uneasy partnership, and after the dismissal of Communist Ministers from government in 1947 (see page 95) the PCF never again joined a coalition. Although de Gaulle's supporters constantly accused the PCF of plotting revolution, it slowly lost its revolutionary fervour.

As support for the big parties sagged, a host of smaller ones appeared – some only lasting one election! Into this rather confusing political arena in the mid-1950s burst Pierre Poujade, a small shopkeeper of St Céré in southern France. When the government in Paris proposed to tighten up on tax evasion, Poujade organised a most bizarre campaign to oppose tax inspectors examining the accounts of a million or so small shops, bars and cafés in France. He immediately became very popular, especially in areas not touched by the boom in trade and industry. In the 1956 elections one commentator wrote, 'Over great tracts of the impoverished south, Poujade ravaged the followings of every party.' $2\frac{1}{2}$ million voters put fifty-three 'Poujadists' into the National Assembly.

But Poujade and his party of the extreme Right had no real policies. His supporters were merely expressing contempt for traditional politicians and The System. In the Assembly the fifty-three deputies put forward no reforms. One deputy of another small party was disgusted – 'Poujadists', he said, 'were incapable of drafting a bill or even of delivering a speech.' In a France grappling with domestic change and colonial conflict, Poujade was not the man of the moment.

NATO and the Common Market

Despite the shifting sands of party support, the Fourth Republic's achievements in European international relations were impressive. Over ten years France played a significant role in building powerful institutions for European security and trade. French statesmen recognised that the days when France could pursue an independent defence policy were over. The fear in western Europe of Soviet Russian expansion was very real; Winston Churchill had proclaimed the sinister existence of an 'iron curtain' across central Europe behind which Russian power steadily increased. In April 1949 France signed a treaty with other western European countries and the United States to form NATO, the North Atlantic Treaty Organisation, whose Article 5 said, 'an armed attack against one or more members shall be considered an attack on them all.' However, when the British Prime Minister, Winston Churchill, proposed to form a European Army, the French Assembly blocked it for four years and finally rejected it. It involved, the deputies said, too great a sacrifice of sovereignty – French soldiers must be under French control.

Trade was a less delicate matter than loss of independence over defence. So the 1950s saw the ideas of Robert Schuman, one of the great statesmen of twentieth-century France, gradually taking shape. First, Schuman suggested the idea of European economic cooperation; then he set up a series of negotiations for six west European nations to cooperate in a 'common market' of coal, iron and steel. It began in 1953, and was an instant success. Then, in March 1957, a wider and more general trading agreement, the EEC (European Economic Community or Common Market), was launched. The treaty said it was to establish 'an enduring and closer union between peoples', but, as with the defence negotiations, sovereignty was ultimately at stake. In the 1960s both NATO and the EEC were to raise awkward questions of sovereignty for the French. But by then the Fourth Republic would be dead.

Dien Bien Phu – the Shock of Decolonisation

Many Frenchmen felt that the Third Republic in the heyday of *la belle époque* deserved credit for gaining an empire. The Fourth Republic had all the odium of losing it. The story was long and tragic, full of contrasting human behaviour – heroism matched with torture, high principles with deceit and treachery.

In the great Age of Imperialism at the end of the nineteenth century people had believed that countries like France, Britain and Germany could, at the same time as increasing their national prestige, offer civilisation and technology to under-developed parts of the world. The Second World War shattered all this. Whatever good the Europeans were doing – in trade unions, education, industrial and agricultural development – they were not doing it fast enough, and certain leaders among the colonial people demanded independence.

Indo-China showed all the best and all the worst in the French handling of her colonies. When it was liberated from Japanese control in 1945, the coastal strip, called Vietnam, already had a leader, Ho Chi Minh, whose communist organisation had been formed in 1941. The French army commander, General Leclerc, decided to be as flexible as possible. He was given a fairly free hand by Paris, and early in 1946 the two men signed an agreement. By it Ho would gain virtually a 'free state' and complete Home Rule. The grim tale of French and later American involvement in Vietnam over the next twenty-five years might never had taken place had Leclerc had his way. But extremists in the French army and diplomatic corps under Admiral d'Argeulieu plotted to regain complete control of Vietnam. On 23 November 1946 French troops invaded Vietnamese areas of Hanoi, the northern capital. From now on no more bargains were possible, and for eight years the struggle went on, played out in the swamps and jungles of the area. The cost in money and men was appalling – there was on average one French officer killed every day of the war, in what one colonel reckoned was 'the graveyard of our army'. Yet the politicians could find no way of ending a hopeless struggle.

Total disaster came to the French early in 1954 at Dien Bien Phu, one of the decisive battles of the twentieth century. Here, in a fifty-six-day siege the French army and the communist Vietminh forces under General Giap fought for control of northern Vietnam. The place was deliberately chosen by the French in a parachute drop of 13,000 soliders well to the rear of the Vietminh. The aim was to tempt groups of the enemy down from their guerrilla hideouts in the surrounding hills and then destroy them piecemeal. It went horribly wrong. Giap did not send his troops in small groups. He sent 50,000 of them to lay siege, and then brought up artillery, something the French commander, General Navarre, thought impossible in the jungle conditions and with French planes raiding Giap's supply lines. In this lay the clue to the disaster. Giap won the battle because he solved the logistical problem of getting supplies through 800 kilometres of jungle, swamps and blown bridges. He used 20,000 coolies from the villages to make a tough, bicycle-pushing human supply column – each man capable of carrying 200 kilogrammes of equipment. For the really heavy material he used 600 Russian-built $2\frac{1}{2}$-tonne trucks. To avoid aerial attack the Vietnamese peasants tied the tops of the trees together to provide a leafy corridor hidden from the pilots above. The French could do little and on 7 May 1954 they gave up. In the falling light of that day the French made their way through deep mud, past mounds of rotting dead and over foul-smelling trenches to Giap's lines.

French reinforcements landing by parachute at Dien Bien Phu in 1954. Enemy communist forces command the area from the hills in the background

Dien Bien Phu proved that it was no longer possible for any democratically-elected government to hold a colony by force in the mid-twentieth century. The whole war had cost France 95,000 men, and Premier Pierre Mendès-France was determined to end it. Late in 1954, at Geneva, he, Eden and Molotov (the British and Russian foreign secretaries) hammered out a settlement. It gave Ho Chi Minh control over North Vietnam, allowed the French to continue trading there, and required a general election to take place in both the North and South zones within two years. The problem of this election brought the Americans to Vietnam in a vain, twenty-year struggle to prevent communist expansion. But it was no longer France's war.

France's African colonies were also pressing for independence. A rebellion in Madagascar in 1947 had been severely repressed, and 'Black Africa' stayed quiet for some years. But the lesson of Dien Bien Phu was not lost on either France or the colonial leaders. Moroccan and Tunisian demands were met by reform not force. By 1956 both were independent, and it was clear that within a few years the rest of French Equatorial Africa would gradually become independent . . .

. . . except Algeria. This country so bedevilled French politics that it eventually destroyed the Fourth Republic.

16
Algeria and the Return of de Gaulle

The Algerian Question

Algeria in the 1950s was quite different from other parts of the French Empire. First, the million or so French settlers had been there twice as long as in, say, Indo-China or Tunisia. Five-sixths of these settlers, or *colons*, had been born there, yet they kept close ties with France, electing members to the National Assembly, and attracting considerable money and effort in Algeria for road-building, health and farming schemes. Apart from the handful of rich landowning *colons*, there were many small farmers, postmen, office workers and railwaymen. These *colons* were afraid of a second aspect of the Algerian question: the growing Moslem population. By 1960 half of Algeria's 8 million Moslems were under twenty years old. They had difficulty in finding work, and their numbers created much unrest both in Algeria and in France, where many migrated in search of jobs. Thirdly, the French army looked on Algeria as their last imperial stronghold. Many soldiers returning from Indo-China were stationed in Algeria, and their officers were determined that France should keep it at all costs. Some French civilians felt the same, especially when oil was discovered in the Saharan interior.

The 8 million Moslem natives had for a long time resented the ruling *colon* élite. The tension snapped late in 1954, when an Algerian Moslem independence movement, the FLN, began guerrilla warfare against French rule. Soon its actions were described in the press in Paris and abroad as 'a cruel, fanatical Arab holy war, a war of hide-and-seek in hill and desert'. By 1955 170,000 French soldiers were fighting in the struggle; within two more years the number had risen to 350,000. The FLN had only 15,000 active soldiers, but they were expert in ambush warfare, had the sympathy of many of the local people, and were difficult to find in the mountainous interior. The contest then turned into that scourge of the twentieth century, an urban guerrilla war, of bombs at bus stops, dance-halls and shopping centres, of mutilations and stabbings of men, women and children. Some French army units met terror with counter-terror, and General Massu's crack 10th Parachute Division gained an unenviable reputation for ruthlessness and torture. The help the FLN were getting from neighbouring countries made things worse for the French. There was world-wide publicity in February 1957 when French planes bombed Sakhiet, inside the Tunisian border, where it was suspected that FLN guerrillas were being harboured: half of the seventy-five people killed in the raid were children.

At home the governments of the Fourth Republic regarded Algeria as a political hot potato. Should they grant concessions to the Moslem 'second-class' citizens? Should they vigorously support the *colons* in the army campaign against terrorism? It seemed impossible to do both at once. Guy Mollet, the Socialist premier, told the Moslems early in 1956, 'I recognise the injustices you have known', but, when he visited Algiers, he was pelted with eggs and rotten tomatoes by *colon* demonstrators. Mollet beat a retreat: he promised a policy of stern resistance to terrorism rather than concessions.

The war dragged on. By early 1958 it had become extremely unpopular in France, yet no government could find an answer. The cost was now £2,000,000 *a day*, money which could have been spent on urgent domestic social reforms. French people were uneasy at the rumours of torture by their army. It was no longer a professional soldiers' war either: young conscripts were being posted to Algeria, and 7,000 had died there already. French international influence was suffering badly. With her army tied up in Algeria she could take no positive role in European affairs; and in 1956 one of her motives in joining Britain in a military onslaught on Egypt had been because President Nasser gave encouragement to the FLN. The worst effect of the war was on French politics. It became increasingly obvious that France would not get a stable government until a solution had been found to the Algerian question. In the autumn of 1957 France was without a government for five weeks, and in April 1958 there was none for four weeks.

On 13 May 1958 Premier Pflimlin, a man known to be in favour of bargaining with the FLN, was due to announce his new cabinet for approval by the Assembly. The next fortnight produced a crisis, the like of which France had not known since 1940.

1958

The *colons* and army officers knew that if Pflimlin was accepted by the Assembly he would soon begin negotiations with the FLN and they were very much afraid that Algeria would be given independence. So on 13 May the generals together with influential *colons* decided to seize power in Algeria and defy the government in Paris. They planned to move at 8 pm. Other groups too were anxious to voice their opinion. Around 6 pm students and other *colons* demonstrated and successfully invaded the government building in Algiers, to destroy they declared, 'the rotten regime'. The generals were angry that 'their' revolt had been taken over but they could do little except move in quickly and assume the leadership. Two of them, generals Massu and Salan, emerged as the guiding spirits.

Meanwhile in Paris, Pflimlin's newly approved government found itself in a difficult situation. His cabinet met urgently, said one of its members, 'resolved to smash the revolt'. Such brave words did little to help, and, as the days wore on, the government became gripped with panicky fears. The army chief of staff in France resigned. In the provinces the prefect at Toulouse told Paris officials, 'We are sitting on a volcano.' Rumours spread that the government was thinking of arming the miners! Many Frenchmen feared France was on the brink of civil war. When news came on 23 May that rebel parachutists had seized Corsica, urgent decisions were sought in Paris.

De Gaulle suddenly attracted support, even from his political enemies. He had taken no part in the crisis; in fact, he had played no active part in the political life of the Fourth Republic since 1946. On 15 May, however, he had announced his 'readiness if called on' – then maintained a masterly silence. To his supporters, he was the man who would give France strong presidential government, vital in seeking a permanent solution to the Algerian question; to his opponents he was the lesser-evil, a temporary answer to a crisis which seriously threatened law and order; to the soldiers, especially the colonels and generals in Algeria, he was 'an army man', who was bound to preserve 'l'Algerie française'.

On 29 May President Coty accepted Premier Pflimlin's resignation. On the radio Coty announced, 'We are on the edge of civil war', and said he had asked de Gaulle to set up a Government of National Safety. De Gaulle stated his own terms for accepting office: he would rule by decree (i.e. without the National Assembly) for six months; then France would be asked to vote on a new constitution which he would frame. Algeria was not mentioned. De Gaulle wanted power first; only then would he suggest an answer. The Fourth Republic was dead. All that remained was to bury it.

Algeria and France calmed down, waiting to see whether de Gaulle would be the new strong man of French politics, a Napoleon or a

Clemenceau. A few months later, in September, one of the most remarkable national referenda in French history took place. Eighty per cent of Frenchmen accepted de Gaulle's new Fifth Republic, with its constitution giving real power to the president and his personal choice of ministers.[1] The days of the all-powerful National Assembly of the Third and Fourth Republics were gone. In the elections for a new Assembly with its much reduced powers, Gaullists swept the board. The great Radical Party was reduced to a mere 37 seats; the Communists were almost wiped out, their 145 seats of 1956 being reduced to 10.

De Gaulle on the Algerian Tightrope

In Algeria FLN terrorism continued sporadically but the army and the *colons* were prepared to wait and see. What they wanted was a clear statement that Algeria would remain part of France forever. Slowly they became disillusioned. De Gaulle would not be drawn. He bought time with vague remarks, but he could not sit on the fence too long. On 16 September 1959 he made a definite promise: 'I undertake to ask Algerians what they wish to be.'

This was too much for some die-hard *colons*, who created an armed demonstration in January 1960. It was poorly organised and easily dealt with by the police. The soldiers there, however, were planning something more spectacular. When de Gaulle finally came out into the open – 'We must disengage from Algeria', he said in April 1961 – the generals, led by Challe and Salan, seized power once again in Algeria. Would 1958 repeat itself? Would de Gaulle go as Pflimlin had gone?

Outwardly, it seemed as serious a crisis as before. The government in Paris was being challenged by a powerful army-led revolt in Algiers. For a while all was uncertainty. De Gaulle appeared on television, dramatically calling on 'the French army to do its duty'. Rumours spread that parachutists were about to land in Paris. Could one old man, making dramatic speeches from a TV screen, work a miracle?

The reality was somewhat different from 1958. De Gaulle's personal authority in France had grown considerably, and people were overwhelmingly hostile to the army rebels. In Algeria Challe was dismayed to find he had no support from the rank-and-file conscript soldiers, on whom he depended. After four days he gave in. Salan, however, quietly disappeared, to organise a secret terrorist army of his

[1]See the guide on page 14

own, the OAS. Car bombs in Algiers and Paris once more created noise, panic and nervousness. In six weeks, late in 1961, there were 314 'bombings' in France; in one town in Algeria, thirty were recorded in one day. But it was no longer the old war. In a quite extraordinary reversal of alliances, the *colon* extremists and Salan's OAS were now France's enemy; meanwhile the FLN and the official French army tried to avoid provoking each other as talks for a peace settlement began.

Finally, at Evian, in south-east France, the tragedy of Algeria was brought to a close. A cease-fire, agreed for 19 March 1962, was to be followed by independence for Algeria, on condition that French oil interests were protected. The nightmare was over, and ninety-one per cent of Frenchmen voted for de Gaulle's settlement. OAS terrorism slowly became less frequent – the cause now seemed forlorn – though there were three attempts to assassinate de Gaulle. And 800,000 *colon* 'refugees' moved back to France, and settled down very quickly.

Algiers, 23 April 1961: a main street scene shows the rebel parachute regiments under Generals Salan and Challe awaiting French government reaction to their seizure of power

Prestige

At the beginning of his war memoirs de Gaulle wrote, 'France cannot be France without greatness.' Now that she had lost all her colonies, de Gaulle, with vigorous leadership and a thriving economy, sought a new role for his nation in world affairs. Leadership of Europe was the prize. De Gaulle's priority was to establish good relations with the old enemy, West Germany. State visits of Chancellor Adenauer to France and of President de Gaulle to Germany led to a Treaty of Cooperation, signed in January 1963. De Gaulle hoped that in future the Germans would accept his guidance from Paris in any difficult international problems. His people were more doubtful. *Le Monde* commented, 'German crowds applauded de Gaulle – better a French general than a Bavarian corporal [i.e. Hitler]. But all this is fragile.' Adenauer soon retired, and de Gaulle had to admit that West Germany had a more fruitful relationship with America than with France. Within months he was lamenting that, 'treaties, like roses, fade'.

In his search for prestige, relations with Great Britain also became difficult – but this was a calculated policy. The ideal of cooperation based on the 1904 Anglo-French Entente was useful in war time, though even then there were tensions; in peacetime old suspicions re-asserted themselves. The French saw Britain once more as 'perfidious Albion', that untrustworthy nation too keen on safeguarding her own interests and those of her empire. So, when Britain applied for membership of the Common Market in the early 1960s, de Gaulle insisted that if Britain wanted to join the now prosperous economic community of western Europe, she must cut herself off from her Commonwealth and American relationships. Macmillan, the British Prime Minister, had no intention of doing this, and showed it forcefully when Britain and the USA signed a nuclear submarine agreement at Nassau in 1962. De Gaulle's reaction was a sensational press conference on 14 January 1963: '*Non*', he said, Britain could not join the Common Market. Again in 1967 he vetoed a British application to join.

The common factor which prevented de Gaulle establishing good relations on his terms with both West Germany and Britain was the United States. President de Gaulle's anti-American feelings were deep-rooted, full of spite and suspicion. He argued that huge US commercial companies had too much influence in France for his liking. Further, he thought that the United States' friendship with Britain and West Germany was their way of trying to gain influence in

Europe and thus threaten his bid for the leadership of the European Community. De Gaulle had never forgotten that the Americans had refused to recognise him as French leader in the early days of the Second World War. So de Gaulle tried to be as independent of the USA as possible. He refused to allow French generals to be part of a unified NATO army, and he decided to speed up the production of a French nuclear bomb. It meant vast extra expense on defence projects which French prosperity only just made possible. This military policy was only the start of an extensive campaign against the economic, diplomatic and cultural influence of the USA in Europe, which de Gaulle launched in 1963 with the slogan, '*l'Europe européenne*'.

De Gaulle's bid for power and influence in international affairs would have been impossible without two things: first, the surging prosperity of the 'fifties and 'sixties, which gave a sound base for his policies; and, secondly, the average Frenchman's fears of creeping Americanisation, of which de Gaulle's hostility was as much an echo of his countrymen's views as it was a personal crusade.

'The reign of Charles XI'

Charles de Gaulle was a puzzling figure. Someone has suggested that he invented his own character. Certainly he presented a carefully planned image to the world. Twice he could claim to have been the man of the hour: in June 1940, when the few men who came to him in Britain felt that 'with him we shall not be humiliated'; and in May 1958 when he would only take power legally, saying 'I cannot consent to receive power from any other source than the people.' After each event he stressed that he stood for France, and for many Frenchmen he had the distinction of recovering French honour as leader of the Free French in the 1940s and as President in the 1960s. To foreigners he was one of those ghosts of French history, a Henry IV or Napoleon, who appeared when there was a critical need for leadership and authority. It was no accident that de Gaulle chose Joan of Arc's Cross of Lorraine as the symbol of the Free French movement in 1940.

This 'most illustrious of Frenchmen', as President Coty called him in 1958, had two ways of presenting his image. First, he appealed directly to the people. He mistrusted political parties and preferred, on the big issues, to use a referendum. He believed that huge majorities declaring '*Oui*' would carry him to new pinnacles of authority. Secondly, in more humdrum matters he proved himself the master of television, either in dramatic appeals to his people, or in televised press conferences – once called 'the absolute weapon of the Fifth Republic', for they were carefully stage-managed with great ceremonial and planted questions.

De Gaulle had many critics. He had a character that irritated other important people. He could be impatient and arrogant. His famous '*Non*' to Britain's Common Market application was done without consulting his partners in the Community; they were very angry. Winston Churchill remarked that even in the dark, early days of the war the greatest cross he had to bear was the Cross of Lorraine (meaning de Gaulle). His aloofness repelled many; one Resistance leader commented, 'On the chessboard on which he plays, there can be no friendship between the knight that is moved and the hand that moves it.'

The French press were certain that after 1958 he was on the road to becoming a dictator. '*Général Moi*' was a constant nickname. The left-wing French philosopher, Jean-Paul Sartre, delivered a biting attack on de Gaulle when, in September 1958, he wrote of 'the future monarchy of King Charles XI'. Sartre went on, 'I do not believe in God, but had I the duty of choosing between Him and de Gaulle, I would vote for God. He is more modest.' Other critics saw de Gaulle's career as a big bluff. They said he did not really 'free' France in 1944: British and American troops did. They also said he hoodwinked his way to an Algerian settlement. And, though his Presidency coincided with a period of prosperity, the base for it all had been laid in the early 'fifties, when de Gaulle was in retirement.

Despite these criticisms de Gaulle must be credited with a superb sense of timing, and with the creation of a personal image of national unity and national greatness. His career may have seemed to some a gigantic confidence trick, but it was one that deserved to come off.

17
Not Everything Prospered

Farming – the Silent Revolution that Lost its Way

The modernisation programme in the period between the end of the Second World War and 1968 did not proceed at the same pace in all areas of the economy, or in the different regions of France. Those on the edge of change fiercely resented what seemed to be happening at the centre. According to one writer, those who suffered reacted on occasions 'with the wild gestures of drowning men'. Nowhere was this clearer than in rural France, where there was certainly a revolution, but one that was piecemeal and sporadic. These tensions are an important part of the history of modern France.

In the middle of the twentieth century France was the richest agricultural nation in western Europe; her climate, fertile soil, space and output gave her enormous advantages. The rich wheat and cattle farms of the Paris Basin and north-east plains were easily modernised, and by the 1960s were as efficient as any foreign competitors. But there were two 'agricultures' in France. The other was represented by the small farms of much of the rest of the country. Nearly three-quarters of all farms had less than twenty hectares, and of these the average was only ten hectares – in Britain and Denmark at least 100 hectares would be regarded as a more economic size.

The worst problem for these small farms was the movement of country people to the town – begun even before the Second World War. This rural exodus left areas like the Massif Central with an ageing population. Young men left seeking forty-hour working weeks and leisure time in the towns, to get away from a seventy-hour weekly toil on the farm. Girls left to avoid the prospect of a life of drudgery, isolation and inferiority – they rarely wanted to marry even a well-to-do farmer. This drift to the cities was seen as a population haemorrhage which deprived the countryside of its life-blood, leaving behind only the old, the dull and the apathetic.

Another problem was two-fold: the emotional attachment which many peasants had for their own piece of land; and, linked with it, the splitting-up of some areas into tiny plots, as a result of fathers in their wills dividing their land between their sons. (If you fly over parts of

France you can see these minute strips looking rather like a bizarre patchwork quilt. In the Loire Valley one area of 2,000 hectares was split into 48,000 plots.) Even if the government could persuade the peasant that it would be more efficient to exchange his bits and consolidate them (the French call this policy, *remembrement,* meaning literally the piecing together of limbs), he may be suddenly, as one writer put it, 'struck with sentimental horror and refuse to give up the field where his father taught him to plough'.

Since 1945 the government had made all kinds of efforts to resolve this problem as well as to stop the exodus of the young. Monnet's Plan (see page 97) put tractors high on its list of priorities. France had only 37,000 tractors in 1945, yet within fifteen years had 625,000. But they were merely a status symbol to some farmers whose fields were too small for tractors to be used profitably. These farmers ran deeply into debt, and so when the cost of living began rising faster than their incomes they protested blindly. In 1957 angry farmers blocked main roads with tractors. But they had no leader, and nothing came of scores of haphazard demonstrations. Three years later, Amiens was the scene of another riot where farmers armed with pitchforks fought police armed with tear-gas. The government promised reform, but delays caused discontent to mount again.

Old style farming still existed in the 1960s. This aerial picture of a village in the lower Seine Valley shows the separate strips belonging to different farmers

Meanwhile, a new force had appeared among the farmers called the Jacists. They were young Catholic farmers, members of the *Jeunesse Agricole Chrétienne*, annoyed that the Paris bureaucrats had done so little to help the small farmers. The Jacists wanted to educate the whole farming community in modern agricultural techniques and proper accounting methods. When violence broke out yet again, in April 1961, the Jacists gave it better leadership, and presented well-thought-out demands. General agricultural reform was the keynote, not just a wild attempt to halt progress. Disturbances began in Brittany at Pont l'Abbé, where a seasonal glut of vegetables had reduced the farmers' prices to almost nothing. The demonstrators tipped tonnes of potatoes on to the streets, and later blocked the roads with tractors at strategic points all over western France. The farmers had a good case: they pointed out that it was the middlemen who made the real profits. Vegetables

Angry tomato growers dump their crop into the River Durance, near Avignon, because of the low price producers received for their goods (often one-tenth of the price paid by Paris consumers)

sold by farmers for 40f a kilo in Brittany would cost the housewife in Paris 300f. Because the artichoke was so often at the centre of the vegetable and fruit price rows those rural disturbances have been nicknamed the 'Artichoke Wars'.

This time de Gaulle's government acted. Edgar Pisani, a tall, black-bearded, flamboyant figure, was appointed to do for agriculture what Monnet had done for industry. The Pisani Law passed in 1961 was a bold first step to haul French farming into the modern world. The government set up pension funds to encourage old farmers to retire early; it lent money to marketing cooperatives; and established SAFERs, or regional agencies, to buy up land as it came onto the market, improve it, and re-sell at moderate prices to young farmers willing to use modern methods. It seemed a rural revolution was on its way at last.

By the 1970s there was much local evidence of change. At Guiche in the Adour Valley in south-west France, the old mayor was proud of the improvements. He said, 'Before 1914 you had to keep tightening belts to live here. They were so poor they used to divide a herring into three parts and an egg into two. Now in 1967 we have cleared and drained more land, extending our acreage from 865 to 1,850 [345 to 740 hectares], and production has doubled.' Elsewhere cooperatives encouraged efficiency. In Beauce, near Paris, one handled eighty per cent of the rich wheat production, storing the considerable surplus, and marketing through good rail links with Italy, Germany and Holland. Its output rose 400 per cent in twenty years. Yet another example of reform was the vast Midi scheme, on the coastal strip west of the Rhône delta. The whole area was made fertile in the 1960s by a far-reaching project of irrigation, water being taken from the Rhône through canals to a pumping station at Nîmes, which fed another network of canals running west. Many neglected vineyards and much marshy land was converted into a fruit farming region for peaches, apples, tomatoes and pears. The Midi scheme might fairly be said to have made a desert bloom.

Despite these changes French farming experts admit that progress has been far too slow. What writers in the 'sixties were promising as a 'silent revolution in the countryside' had somehow lost its way. Examples of efficiency and reform in some places distracted from the more general picture of near-stagnation. In Paris, the Pisani office was kept very short of funds. Schemes involved long official delays: a SAFER idea might take five years to go though lawyers' hands. By 1970 SAFER had handled a mere ten per cent of only that land which had come onto the market. France has over 37,000 villages, each with less than a thousand people, and it was plainly impossible for Jacist or Pisani ideas to get to all of them. The Lozère area of the Massif Central was perhaps the most backward of all France. Peasants living on its poor soil had a patch of vines producing a rather vinegary wine, a few cows and some chickens; they ate meat only once a week; children slept in haylofts, and the working day was regularly sixteen hours. The young moved quickly away from these grim upland hamlets. The government felt there was no future for such areas except as forests and tourist attractions. Lozère might have been the worst, but there were many other areas about which the officials in Paris despaired.

Finally the CAP, or Common Agricultural Policy of the Common Market, has not brought the French farmer all the benefits he hoped for. Basically the CAP works through a levy (or tax) on the food imports to all EEC members, which is then redistributed to farmers in the form of subsidies or guaranteed prices. A country like France which imported very little food did well, yet the money tended to go to the big farms, which were efficient anyway. And so, as the big farms got richer, the smaller farms got poorer. The CAP merely widened the gap between the two 'agricultures' of France.

Old Craft Traditions

Whilst much of French industry was booming, there were a great many small enterprises which hardly changed. What they produced was fine, but they were, so to speak, craftsmen of quality in an age wanting quantity. For instance, France had 18,000 furniture firms in the 'sixties, 17,000 of them employing fewer than ten workers. One town illustrates the general problem. Thiers is a small country town of 20,000 people in the Auvergne area of central France. Its nickname was 'the French Sheffield', but it had no large factories. The main streets were lined with 250 tiny, rather dingy, workshops producing thousands of kinds of cutlery. In some of them old men had spent a working life lying on their stomachs polishing knives. Despite government encouragement the craftsmen were unwilling to modernise – they said they would rather work independently in their own time than be 'well-paid slaves' in a factory.

Housing Neglect

The story of French housing was a sorry tale of neglect from 1914 to about 1954. Rents, frozen in the First World War to prevent landlords profiteering, remained roughly the same afterwards. Very little profit could be made from tenants, so no one was willing to invest in building programmes, except big houses for the well-to-do. Britain built twice as many houses as France in the same period, yet she only had a fraction of the damage suffered by France in two world wars. State housing (the main kind were called HLMs, a kind of council house block) began on a large scale only in the late 'fifties. By 1970, 15 million people had been rehoused. But housing had been neglected for so long that there were huge waiting-lists, and there were few state mortgages to enable the young *bourgeoisie* to buy houses. Only in the 1960s did the French attempt building society schemes like those which operated in other countries such as Britain. One long-held French tradition made things worse: people preferred to live in or close by a city rather than commute long distances to work. This made building land scarce and there was much competition which made prices rise. Between 1945 and 1957 houses around many cities increased twenty-fold; and in 1970 a square metre of land on the Champs Elysées in Paris could cost up to 10,000 francs. Suspicion of corruption in government circles prompted *Le Monde* to say in 1965, 'The State's connivance at [tolerance of] land speculation shows a crisis of morality in high places.' Some of the architecture too has been criticised. Cheap, almost cut-price, HLMs were built at Sarcelles, just outside Paris, in the mid-1960s. An architectural authority labelled it 'a loveless, pre-cast concrete desert'. However, with the general housing shortage most of Sarcelles' inhabitants were, according to a 1968 survey, 'happy to be living there', even if they had to cope with all the problems of high-rise flats.

That 'National Disaster', the French Telephone System

The French telephone system had a terrible record in the 'fifties and 'sixties. Georges Pompidou, later President of France, was driven to call it a 'national disaster'. His judgement was based on some alarming facts. In the late 'sixties, 600,000 people were on the waiting-list for a telephone; the number of telephone lines per 100 people (just over six) was the worst of any industrialised country in the world; queues waited impatiently at post offices to make long-distance calls; nearly half of all calls failed to get through the network first time; and in thousands of French villages telephone operators insisted on shutting down during the night and during a two-hour lunch break. Reform of the system did not appear in any of Monnet's schemes, and the press reckoned that de

Gaulle's prestige projects took money that should have been used to improve the system. Only in the 1970s did the government make an effort to increase the number of lines.

A Social Problem Called Vin Rouge

France has 1,300,000 vinegrowers, and her best wines (efficiently graded and labelled *appellation contrôlée*) like Burgundy, Bordeaux and Beaujolais, have had a high international reputation. Medium quality wines (labelled VDQS) also formed an increasingly important part of the home and overseas market. The rest, *vin ordinaire,* much of it simply called *rouge*, was extremely cheap, and drunk by Frenchmen in great quantities. The government launched a campaign in 1954 to reduce one of France's greatest social problems: alcoholism. Heavy drinking was gradually reduced in the towns, but in the rural areas it was still serious. In 1970 1,700,000 adults were medically classified as alcoholics, and in Brittany the death-rate due in some measure to heavy drinking was eight times the national average – many men there drank five litres of *rouge* a day, whilst doctors suggested one litre a day was a reasonable maximum.

In the twenty years from 1947 to 1967 France underwent a great resurgence in her national life. Yet the fact that some areas of the economy were progressing faster than others, and that some key problems had had insufficient money and attention from government planners created tension. It was in the area of education that tension snapped.

18
1968: Crisis Year

Students: Les Enfants Terribles

France in the early spring of 1968 seemed untroubled, peaceful and prosperous. Yet in a remarkable editorial on 15 March, the highly – respected newspaper, *Le Monde*, complained, 'The French are bored. Youth is bored. The backslapping and preaching of politicians appear comic or pointless. Everyone else is bored. Nothing disturbs the calm.'

Below the surface there were more serious rumblings in the universities. The university authorities seemed utterly remote to most students. Lecturers expressed surprise if anyone asked a question, and students resented the stress laid on memorising vast quantities of facts and on mastering complex literary techniques. The average student was also indignant about the few élite colleges called the *Grandes Écoles*. Their prestige, conditions of work and excellent career prospects made places in them much sought after prizes. The two with the best reputation, the École Polytéchnique (a creation of Napoleon I) and the Normale Supérieure, stood in the centre of Paris like bastions of privilege to a struggling university student at, say, the nearby science department of the Sorbonne.

The worst problem was one of numbers. In 1939 France had 120,000 students; this had risen by 1960 to 250,000; by 1968 the figure was a staggering 612,000. In Paris the Sorbonne University alone had 160,000; in the provinces, Caën University, for example, had ten times as many students as it had in 1939. These large numbers caused important problems. Efficient lecturers were hard to find. A lecture-hall for 500 was often crammed with 1,000. There were few state grants for students (only twenty-two per cent had them, and these were low), so most students worked part-time or even full-time in jobs. The 'drop-out' rate was alarming: sixty per cent of a year's entry failed to complete the course and take a degree. Many of these were not serious students, either because they had enrolled as a kind of status symbol, or, as some girls admitted, they came to find a husband; others simply were not clever enough for advanced study.

The reason for these enormous numbers was the rapid rise in the birthrate coupled with the rule in France that anyone passing his *baccalauréat* examination (the leaving test of the *lycée* or French high school) could enter a university. The effect of all this on most students was anxiety, frustration and often boredom. A minority turned to revolutionary action.

Revolt

It began at Nanterre. Described by one lecturer as 'a gleaming block of plate-glass and concrete standing in the middle of a waste lot', this was an over-spill college of the Sorbonne, set in the distant north-west suburbs of Paris. Here Daniel Cohn-Bendit and a few social science students formed a 'Red and Black' left-wing group, intent on political action. In late March 1968 they attempted to disrupt some university examinations on the grounds that 'they rewarded only those who co-operated with the system'. They held debates on 'the struggles of

Students hurling missiles in a main street in Paris in May 1968; the CRS, French riot police, are replying with CS Gas-bombs

the working class'. A few weeks later rival left-wing groups clashed. But the big occasion was 1 May, when the authorities sensed trouble as 50,000 students and others marched through Paris on a May-Day demonstration. The next day the authorities closed Nanterre, and the head of the university asked for police help.

Up to this point the university authorities had first ignored the general student complaints, then acted rather hastily against the small, local left-wing group of Cohn-Bendit. Within a week this local incident had grown into a mass movement of virtually all students in Paris, with huge public support and much sympathy from provincial students. Their clashes with the police intensified and they set up barricades in the student area of central Paris, the Quartier Latin. On 6 May 600 students and 345 police were wounded in a riot. The Sorbonne itself was closed on the 9 May. On the night of 10–11 May a long, bloody battle took place over the sixty barricades which criss-crossed the student area, police, tear-gas and incendiary bombs being met by students' cobble stones and Molotov cocktails (petrol bombs in bottles). There were 367 serious casualties and 188 cars were destroyed. The next day, all over France – at Strasbourg, Rennes, Bordeaux – university premises were 'occupied' by students. Some university lecturers, including three Nobel Prize winners, joined the student cause.

So far the government, and particularly de Gaulle, had made only occasional comments. They were clearly unprepared and very much on the defensive. As the government 'retreated' so others moved in to support the students. There were many in France who disliked de Gaulle's authoritarian leadership. On Monday 13 May factory workers entered the struggle with wage demands. A one-day General Strike was called. Immense crowds demonstrated in Paris, three-quarters of a million people thronging the boulevards. This time the police stayed away. During the next week there were strikes throughout industry. Starting at the Sud-Aviation works at Nantes, they spread to the Renault factories at Cléon, Flins, Le Mans and Billancourt. The students, meanwhile, kept up their pressure to 'boycott the exams'. The strikes then hit important publicly-owned industries. The railways joined in. The Paris Central Postal Sorting Office closed. Teachers went on strike. By the 20 May the Paris stock-exchange, the Bourse, ceased business. Long queues developed at petrol stations, at the banks, and outside food shops. Within days they too closed down. On the 24 May ORTF (French television) staff went on strike, and the same day witnessed the fiercest battles of May so far. The Bourse was set on fire, and nearly 1,000 were wounded in further clashes with the CRS, the

French riot police.

Mid-May had seen possibly the largest general strike in history, anywhere in the world. The Gaullist government, wrote the historian, Eric Hobsbawm, had been 'caught on the wrong foot at the start and was unable to recover itself'. But who would step into the vacuum left by the progressive crumbling of government authority? The French Communist Party could have taken the chance, but it hesitated. It too had been caught without making adequate plans for seizing power from de Gaulle. Although there were more demonstrations at the end of the month, and cries of 'a people's government' were heard, the revolt slowly ran out of steam. Thursday 30 May proved critical.

De Gaulle, a brilliant political tactician, sensed that the time had come to act. With his opponents – students, workers, the unions, the Communist Party – losing momentum, he played his government's ace: he declared that his authority, and his authority alone, could deal with the spectre of revolution. On the 30 May he dissolved the National Assembly and announced elections for the end of June. 'It was', says one writer, 'a beautifully judged performance. De Gaulle did not even have

The CRS cordoning off parts of the Latin Quarter in Paris in the 1968 student disturbances

to shoot!' He told Frenchmen in clear terms that the issues were no longer student overcrowding or worker-student solidarity to improve wages; the issue was defence against red revolution and its threat of civil war. Many people by now considered that the student and worker extremists had gone too far. Too many cars had been set alight, too many paving-stones ripped up in the battles at the barricades.

Workers began to drift back to the factories. De Gaulle, on television, said he sympathised with the problems of students and accepted the idea of 'participation' – that they should have some voice in their universities' affairs. This cut the ground from under the feet of the more revolutionary students, who clashed with the police again at the Sorbonne on 11 June, but opinion was obviously swinging back to de Gaulle. On 30 June elections showed the left-wing politicians in disarray as de Gaulle's supporters were re-elected with twenty per cent *more* votes than previously. De Gaulle had won. But he was committed to some kind of educational reform, so, for the moderates in the May revolt, all had not been in vain.

Aftermath: Exit de Gaulle 1969

Gradually things returned to normal, but France would never be quite the same again. People examined the lessons, costs and shifts of power that had taken place, and wondered how the country would adapt to the new situation. Wages had risen by thirteen per cent, some of this being the price employers paid to get the workers back. De Gaulle's government had won the election, but its respect had been seriously damaged. As the newspaper *Le Combat* said, 'The country did not by its vote approve Gaullist policy; it simply condemned violence.' Abroad, the *New York Times* saw this when it argued on 1 July: 'The revolt was against the Gaullist régime, its authoritarianism, and its concern with prestige abroad instead of problems at home.'

The revolt had left a trail of difficulties and unanswered questions behind it. The wage increases soon produced inflation and a franc currency crisis. University methods would have to be reformed – but how? 'Participation' was a great rallying cry, but difficult to put into practice. Moreover, lower down the educational ladder, in the schools, there was now mounting pressure to make the emphasis on written examinations less intense.

The most interesting question-mark hung over de Gaulle's own future. The events of May 1968 had a remarkable sequel a year later, when Charles de Gaulle, President of the Fifth Republic, the 'image' of

France for a decade, and a man with an immense international reputation, resigned. The occasion was an April 1969 referendum on regional development, and although it seemed odd that de Gaulle should stake his whole political future on it, he felt he needed a giant national vote of confidence in himself. Strong criticism of his failure to do much after the May crisis hinted also that de Gaulle's creation of a red spectre was quite hollow. The French Communist Party was nothing like as extreme and revolutionary as he had painted it. When it came to the vote it was soon obvious that the old spell of Gaullist authority was broken. He was defeated. He retired from politics, and died in November 1970, just before his eightieth birthday.

19
Change and Continuity in the 1970s

Pompidou and Giscard D'Estaing

De Gaulle's successor as President was Georges Pompidou, who had been a strong Gaullist supporter. For many years people had regarded him as the heir-apparent to the 'reign of Charles de Gaulle', and thus the government stayed broadly right-wing after 1969. Pompidou's task was not an enviable one. One of his early decisions was to bring into his government Valéry Giscard D'Estaing, whose financial talents amounted almost to wizardry. Industrial production and trade continued to prosper, and his skill with the franc meant that France kept inflation down to a reasonable amount – an impressive accomplishment in the early 1970s, when world oil shortages and a trade depression created enormous international difficulties. Giscard himself was to succeed Pompidou as President in the summer of 1974.

Pompidou's task involved a delicate balancing act: he had to allow for a certain amount of social reform to deal with the frustrations of 1968, whilst not upsetting the many powerful conservative right-wingers in France who feared too rapid change. He first struck a bargain with the unions, in which pay rises were guaranteed as a guard against inflation. These rises were called *contrats du progrès* and covered most of the public services and industries; they helped avoid major strikes. Then Pompidou made some concessions to the age-old demand that the provinces of France be given a greater voice in the country's affairs. He took up the idea and declared it to be *'la grande affaire de la nation'*. Industries and the arts were encouraged to move to Bordeaux, Grenoble, Rennes, Lyon, and other big cities. To the dismay of many Frenchmen, however, 'government' with all its power and officials stayed as centralised as ever in Paris.

Pompidou put an end to the glory-hunting ideas of de Gaulle, stating there were to be no more prestige projects like the liner *France* and the Rance tidal-dam. A French official said in 1972, 'We are now trying to cut our cap according to our cloth.' Further, Pompidou considered that oil and nuclear power were menacing aspects of de Gaulle's go-it-alone policy: he was proved right in 1971 when the Algerians nationalised the French oil companies in their country, paying very little compen-

sation to France. So the French had to make some difficult treaty arrangements with the powerful Arab oil states. Pompidou also
introduced a new slogan, 'All electric power to be nuclear', and signed,
in 1971, an agreement with Germany, Britain and Italy that they
should all work together for this aim. The intention was to raise the use
of nuclear power as a source of electricity from three per cent to twenty
per cent in ten years. Pompidou's fourth effort was in university reform.

'Who's got time to run the university?'

Pompidou put Edgar Faure, one of France's ablest politicians, in charge
of educational reform. His problem was to find an acceptable way of
granting students' demands first for some kind of control, free of central
direction from Paris; and secondly, that students should participate in
decision-making at their universities. His answer was to split the larger
universities into smaller blocks (the Sorbonne was divided into
thirteen), and to ask students and staff to form UERs – units of a
thousand or so members roughly grouped according to similar subjects
being studied. 684 of these UERs emerged throughout France, each
electing its own council and drawing up its own rules, teaching
methods, syllabuses and examinations. This was only a start. Faure's
successor grappled with thornier problems and put forward proposals in
1974 for selective entry to university, thus reducing the swelling
numbers. But they were greeted with a storm of protest. Later, in 1976
students began 1968-style demonstrations against a suggestion that
students could only apply for courses which had good job prospects.

Yet many students had become disillusioned with the whole process
of reform. Canteens and lecture-halls were as overcrowded as ever;
grants were still small; the Ministry of Education in Paris kept the
crucial control of finance. Final disenchantment came over participation: four years after the 1968 crisis, only twenty-seven per cent of
students bothered to vote for the councils of the UERs. The rest would
shrug their shoulders and àsk, 'Who's got time to run the university?'

Franglais, c'est OK

The worst contemporary change in the view of some Frenchmen
concerns the invasion of their language by American and British
phrases. It has mainly affected the clothing and cosmetics trade and
some food shops. This mixture of French and 'Anglo-Saxon' words is
called *franglais*. Boutiques named *Le Sweater Shop*, advertisements in

"Watch your language
m'sieur, those two are
plain-clothes men from
the Anti-Franglais squad."

A Punch cartoon of 1976 commenting on the French government's attempts to halt the infiltration of the French language with English words

newspapers for *Le véritable wash-and-wear*, or simply *le shopping* are examples. Fear of Americanisation has been a powerful emotion in France, and gourmets were horrified when in the late 1960s an energetic young caterer, Jacques Borel, opened up a chain of Wimpy Bars in Paris, offering on the menu, *'un wimpy 1.85 francs; avec chips 3 francs; un super-wimpy king-size 3.5 francs; un breakfast anglais 5.75 francs'*. The government tried to get *franglais* banned by law in 1976 but large numbers of Frenchmen are doubtful of its chances.

The Architecture of Paris

Nowhere can the problems of change and continuity in contemporary French society be better seen than in the skyline and thoroughfares of Paris. Paris grew up as a walled city and its buildings were constructed on a very dense pattern – sometimes only ten metres wide yet five storeys high. Georges Haussmann, in the mid-nineteenth century, planned vast improvements to realise Napoleon III's dream 'to make Paris the most beautiful city in the world'. In his famous boulevards he succeeded, but old properties remained behind the new streets, and he merely shifted the overcrowding to the northern and eastern outskirts. Despite some people's criticism of 'the architectural tyranny of the straight line', Haussmann's ideas were admired and copied all over Europe.

Haussmann had eased the traffic-flow in central Paris, but only temporarily. It again reached overwhelming proportions when, in 1882, 36,200 vehicles were counted down Haussmann's Avenue de l'Opéra in one day! Then in 1898 the first line of the *Métro*, Paris's underground railway, was laid, and many thought the city's transport problems were solved. They were disappointed. Within ten years a

Métro official complained, 'It does nothing to reduce surface movement; on the contrary it multiplies it.' People continued to move to Paris from the provinces until by the 1960s there were 42 people to a hectare (the same area in London had only 17).

The government proposed a bold scheme in 1960 called PADOG, which would try to cut down further building and preserve the old skyline of the city. Within two years the government changed its mind. De Gaulle put Paul Delouvrier, a talented civil servant, in charge of a new planned expansion which was meant to revive for Paris its old international reputation. Called the *Schéma*, this thirty-year plan took over PADOG's ideas for renovating central Paris. It added ideas for five new cities to be built on either side of the Seine, and began construction of *La Défense*, a huge new business centre in the western suburbs (its twenty-six office and apartment blocks for 40,000 people tower above the skyline behind the Arc de Triomphe). The *Schéma* was put rapidly into operation. Les Halles, the terribly congested central food market,

La Défense 1975, the vast office building project in western Paris

which handled 6,000 tonnes of fruit and vegetables each day, was shifted to the southern outskirts in 1969. The skyscrapers of *La Défense* began soaring, and a new motorway to encircle the city, the Boulevard Périphérique, was completed in 1972.

Many people criticised the *Schéma*. 'A Gaullist attempt to revive the royal myth of Imperial Paris', cried left-wingers. And that most temperamental Parisian of all, the motorist, complained loudly: 'You may sweep majestically down the Champs-Elysées, then get stuck for half an hour in the bottlenecks between Concorde and the Opéra.' Other people's views were more favourable. 'Paris will perhaps be saved', agreed those Frenchmen who wanted a solution to the nightmare of modern urban congestion.

Partnership and Goodwill

In January 1972 Britain signed the Treaty of Accession in Brussels. After difficult discussions, and with reservations existing on both sides, she joined the Common Market. The enlargement of the EEC had long been an ambition of several members; only France had rigidly refused (twice) to accept Britain's entry. Now, at the third attempt, the governments of Britain (under Edward Heath) and France came to a working agreement. French suspicions that Britain might still 'shop elsewhere' (i.e. trade with the Commonwealth), and fears in Britain, that on entry she would give up some part of her cherished sovereignty, remained. Clearly the entry was an act of faith, that *eventually* something beneficial would come from partnership.

For the Treaty of Accession, like the Anglo-French Entente of 1904, was merely a paper statement. In the end success or failure of the partnership will depend on goodwill and some sympathy for each other's problems. To this end the reader of this book is invited to ponder two remarks:

> '*France is every man's second country.*'
> > (*Thomas Jefferson, President of the United States of America, 1801–1809*)

> '*The French are the most fickle and unmanageable people on earth . . . How can you govern a country that has 246 varieties of cheeses?*'
> > (*Charles de Gaulle, President of France, 1958–1969*)

Index

Algeria, 99; colonisation of, 31; cost of conquest, 29; and de Gaulle, 115–17; struggle for independence, 113–17

Americanisation, 104, 136

Army; health of conscripts (1900s), 37; military complacency (1938), 73

'Beautiful years' (c. 1890–1910), 45–7; arts, 46–7; falsely described, 45; fashions, 45–6; science and technology, 47

Birthrate, 35–6, 104–5

Blum, L., socialist leader, 71–2; and his Matignon Agreement, 72; defines treason (of Pétain), 91

Boulanger, General G., 17–18; and attempted coup, 18

Bourgeoisie, *grande* and *petite*: domination of society, 37–8; and social malaise, 74; *see also* Peasants, Working class

Catholic Church, 43; disestablishment, 45; educational influence, 43–4; social influence, 44

Clemenceau, G., 13, 60–1; dies embittered, 75; and the Dreyfus affair, 23; and w.w.1, 59; and the Paris Commune, 7; at Peace Conference (1919), 59

Colonies and colonisation; after w.w.2, 95–6, 99, 110–17, 118; British/French Entente, 30, 49; by 'men on the spot', 30, 31; faults of, 31–2; foundations of new colonial empire, 28; Galliéni's policy ('splash of oil'), 31; loss of old empire, 28; major areas of expansion, 29–30; North African acquisitions, 29; political and public antipathy, 31: *see also*: Ferry, J.; Algeria: Indo-China

Daladier, E; appeases Hitler, 73

De Gaulle, C., 74, 79, 80, 105, 134: and agriculture, 124; and Algeria, 124; described variously, 119–20; hostility to former allies, 118–19; and liberation 90–1, 93; organises resistance, 87–9; and politics, 107; resigns Presidency, 94; and students'/ civil disorders, 130–2; war memoirs, 118; final resignation and death,

132–3

De Lesseps, F. 18, 29

Dreyfus, Captain A., 19, 20–1, 24; arrest of, 20; his retrial, 25–6; innocence established, 27; pardoned, 27; sentences, 21, 26; *see also* Dreyfus affair

Dreyfus affair, 19, 44; circumstances leading to, 19–20; Clemenceau's involvement, 23; doubts and new evidence, 21–2; Emile Zola's involvement, 23; fresh investigations, 22; the guilty parties, 27; new evidence confirmed, 25; personalities involved, 19; *see also* Dreyfus, A.,

Economy, the: after w.w.1, 60–1; compared to Britain and Germany, 35; decline (1938), 75–6; the Depression (1931) 67; development (1946–67), 97–107; Marshall Plan aid, 97–9; Monnet Plan, 97–9; progress (late 1920s), 65–6; prospects (c. 1900), 33–5, (1947) 95–6; reforms by Pompidou, 134; and German reparations (1919), 61–2, 64–5

Education; conflict between State and Church, 43–5; numbers of students (1968), 128; reforms, 132, 135; students' revolt (1968), 129–30

Empire, *see* Colonies

Energy resources, 101–2

European Economic Community, 109; Britain's entry, 138; and Schumann, 109; veto of Britain's application, 118

Farming and agriculture; (1944–68), 121–5; continuing difficulties, 124–5; dissatisfaction of farmers, 122–3; improvement under de Gaulle, 124; and Monnet's Plan, 122; modernisation, 121

Ferry, J., 13; colonial vision upheld, 31; and republican control of Assembly 16; colonial policy, 29, 30, 31

First World War (w.w.1); cause, 48–9; early hostilities, 50–3; final victory, 59, 60; Foch's new strategy, 59; French preparations, 50; French recovery, 51–3; German preparations, 49, 50; reparations from Germany,

61–3; soldiers' discontent, 56–8; trench warfare, 53–5; Verdun, 55–6; *see also* Germany

Foch, Marshall, C-in-C Allied armies (w.w.1), 59

Fourth Republic, 93–4; and de Gaulle, 93–4; downfall, 115; its founding, 94; international influence, 109

Franco-Prussian War, 1–4; armistice, 3, 4; continued resistance, 3; defence and surrender of Paris, 3

French politics, a guide, 14–15

Gambetta, L., 2, 3, 13, 16, 43
General strike (1968), 130–1
Germany: colonial challenge, 30; invasion of France (w.w.2), 77–82; occupation of N. France, 84, 86–7; reparations to France (w.w.1), 61–3; and Vichy government, 84–7; *see also*; w.w.1; w.w.2

Giscard d'Estaing, V. 134

Hitler, A., 68, 73, 75, 79, 118
Housing, 125–6

Imperialism, *see* Colonies
Indo-China, 95, 99; its loss, 110–12; *see also* Colonies
Inflation (1920s), 63–5

Napoleon III, captured at Sedan, 1
North Atlantic Treaty Organisation (NATO), 109

Paris: defence and surrender (1870), 3; captured (1940), 81; liberation (1944), 91; redevelopment, 136–8
Paris Commune (1871): its beginnings, 5; different ideals, 7–8; elections for council, 7; exiled Communards return, 16; reasons for setting up, 5; suppression and aftermath, 9–10
Peasants: Karl Marx's view of, 39; living conditions, 38–9; *see also* Working class,
Pétain, Marshall, 83; at Verdun, 55; as C-in-C French army (w.w.1), 57; head of Vichy Govt., 84, 85–6; his trial, 91–2; and w.w.2 armistice, 82
Poincaré, R., 75; and German reparations (w.w.1), 63; and inflation (1920s), 65
Politics and politicians: and de Gaulle, 107; general antipathy, 41–2, 107;

guide to Fr. politics, 14–15; the parties (1945) 107–9; corruption/ instability, 68, 75; the 'Left' and 'Right', 42; Left-wing organisations, 71–3; political scene (1900) 42–3, (1947) 107; Right-wing organisations, 69–70

Pompidou, G.: de Gaulle's successor, 134; promotes social/economic reforms, 134

Schumann, R., architect of E.E.C., 109
Second Fr. Empire, 1
Second World War (w.w.2), 76, 77–81; armistice (reasons for/events leading to), 81–3; Fr. anti-invasion plans, 77; German invasion, 77–82; German occupation, 84, 86–7; liberation, 90–2; partisan resistance, 87–9, 90; post-war legacy 94–5; *see also*: Germany; Vichy Govt.

Social classes, *see*: Bourgeoisie; Peasants; Working class
Stavisky, S. A., and corruption in politics, 68–9
Student's revolt (1968), 129–30; aims achieved, 132; consequences, 132–3; leads to civil disturbances, 130–2

Third Republic, 2; approved by electorate, 13; at Bordeaux, 5, 11; at Versailles, 5; attempted coups, (1886) 17, (1934) 70–1; becomes republican, 12; downfall, 76, 84, 85; elections, 3; legally established, 12; no legality (1870), 11; republican or monarchist?, 11; social reforms, 16; taxation, 41
Thiers, A., 1st leader of Third Rep., 2, 3, 11, 12; and Paris Commune, 6–10
Trade unions (1890s), 40
Transport and communications (1946–76), 99–101

Vichy France, 84–9; collaboration policy, 86; and P. Laval, 85, 86, 88, 91–2; resistance to, 87–9; *see also*: Germany; Pétain
Vietnam, *see* Indo-China

Wine, a social problem, 127
Working class (industrial); conditions of work, 39–40; trade unions, 40; views of bourgeoisie, 39

Zola, E. 23–4, 39